ENDORSEMENTS

There are such a wide range of reasons to get help from a consultant and an equally wide range of consultants to choose from. *Stop Wasting Money on the Wrong Consultant* makes the process of knowing what to do really easy so you can make the right decisions for your company.

~ Kevin Rabbitt, CEO, NEP Group

During my career I've worked with a variety of consultants and have acted as a consultant myself, and found this book to have many eye-opening insights and helpful thoughts. When you know how to select and then manage the relationship with your consultants, you can expect enormous returns—*Stop Wasting Money on The Wrong Consultant* by Pete Winiarski will help you do exactly that.

~ Dick Ryan, Lean Journey Leader, Barry Wehmiller Companies

This book has proven to be tremendously useful. *Stop Wasting Money on the Wrong Consultant* has everything you need to know to find the perfect consultant to guide you to higher profits, an engaged workforce, and sustainable results. Read this book!

~ John Uliano, COO, C&M Corporation

Pete Winiarski has hit a home run with *Stop Wasting Money on the Wrong Consultant*. When you discover from reading this book how to pick the right consultant for your business and find the best way to leverage that consultant to solve your biggest problems and hit your biggest goals, you will be happy about the tons of value they deliver and a huge ROI that will come your way.

~ Terri Levine, Co-Founder of The Business Consultant Institute and Best-Selling Author of The Ultimate Game Plan: Power Up Your Consulting Business and Skyrocket Your Revenues *and of* Turbocharge: How to Transform Your Business as a Heart-repreneur®

We have used consultants for a variety of purposes over the years. When you have the right consultant to guide you, you can augment your team's capabilities, build engagement, and get the results you need. This book helps you understand the many consulting choices you have and walks you through exactly what you can do to ensure your consulting engagements yield the highest possible results.

~ Jeff Brubaker, SVP Operations Services, Consolidated Container Corporation

This is a terrific guidebook about how to engage consultants. Even if you have worked with consultants before, Pete Winiarski shares some beneficial insights for you to make your next project even more successful.

~ Joseph Goding, COO, Aegis Energy Services, Inc.

I wish I had this book when we began our strategy execution! *Stop Wasting Money on the Wrong Consultant* simplifies the process and is the ultimate guide for finding, understanding, and working with consultants. Pay close attention to the common business reasons for consulting support, the various misconceptions about consultants, and the myriad of insights this book will give you—you'll be glad you have this book to steer you.

~ Peter Paindiris, President, Teknikor Contracting

I've been a Private Equity Operating Partner working with portfolio companies, a management consultant, and now I'm an executive at a fast growing company. In all these roles, I've spent a lot of time hiring and working with consultants, with varying degrees of success. This book is a helpful summary of how to ensure a positive impact. I wish I'd had it years ago to give to executives, and I'm excited to start using it now with my teams.

~ Yvonne Hao, COO/ CFO at PillPack

Save yourself from learning lessons the hard way. *Stop Wasting Money on the Wrong Consultants* will teach you what you need to know to make the most of your investment in consulting support.

~ Brian Montanari, CEO, Habco Industries

During my career, I have had the pleasure to hire and interact with many large and small consulting firms. Finding the right consultant for the different businesses I ran was one key to us hitting our goals faster than if we tried to do it on our own. Pete Winiarski has made understanding the consulting process easy in this straightforward book. Read it now and follow his advice, and you will greatly improve the success of your consulting projects.

~ Art Byrne, Operating Partner, J.W. Childs Associates, former CEO of Wiremold, and author of The Lean Turnaround

Throughout my career, I have worked with consulting firms specializing in operations, supply chain, marketing, and information technology. Over forty years I have learned the first step to assure success of the project is having clear understanding of what you are trying to accomplish and then to assess the capabilities of the consulting firm and process to achieve these goals. In this book, Pete Winiarski helps you understand what to look for in your consultants, identifies the key elements of the engagement process that you need to have in place, and helps you to improve outcomes by following his framework. Next time your best first step may be reading this book!

~ Neal J. Keating, Chairman, President & Chief Executive Officer, Kaman Corporation

This is a must-read book for business leaders who are considering hiring consultants. In this fast and easy read, *Stop Wasting Money on the Wrong Consultant* will get you quickly up to speed so you can make better decisions, partner up with the best consultant for you, and know how to build a solid and lasting relationship with your consultant so you can exceed your goals.

~ Evan Berns, CEO, Seitz LLC

As someone who wants to get a positive return on investment on every dollar spent, I appreciate the insight and practical information in Pete Winiarski's book, *Stop Wasting Money on the Wrong Consultant*, to help guide business transformation in complex environments. Once again, Pete has added to his growing library of books a valuable resource for management teams. His new book hits the mark.

~ Rodney Glass, SVP and Chief Operating Officer, HID Global

I was a consultant before I ran businesses and hired them to help me. This book reveals many of the unknown secrets about consulting and teaches you exactly what you need to know so you can pick the right one and truly enjoy a huge ROI with their help. When you're ready to get help from consultants, grab this book.

~ Felix Oliha, Operations Excellence Leader for multiple billion $ global companies and Independent Consultant for McKinsey and Company's Operations Practice

STOP WASTING MONEY ON THE WRONG CONSULTANT

STOP WASTING MONEY ON THE WRONG CONSULTANT

How to Pick the Right Consultant to Create Huge Profits and Long-term ROI

Pete Winiarski

WIN
Publishing, LLC

Published by Win Publishing, LLC
35 East Main Street
Suite 337
Avon CT, 06001

ISBN-13: 9780982686539
ISBN-10: 0982686536

Contents

Acknowledgements

As with every book I've written so far, I think about my family above anything else. My wife, Marie, and sons, Nicholas and Nathan, I want you to know that even when I'm working late hours or bring my laptop with me on vacation so that I can catch a little time early before we start our adventures—I am doing this with you on my mind. Thank you for putting up with my crazy schedule and my passion to help people.

Of course, running the day-to-day operations in my consulting company is a challenge with such huge projects as writing and publishing another book. That is why I love my team so much. David Tweedt—you keep our extended team engaged and our clients thrilled with our support. Kelly Bluestein and Christina Orlich—you keep all the administrative details working smoothly and our various projects moving forward so that I don't have to worry about the details. Thank you! I have so much fun with you all and love the impact we have in the world—always remember that you are critical to helping make this happen.

I want to acknowledge Terri Levine, my business partner in my other company, the Business Consultant Institute. Before we joined forces there, it was Terri's idea to create a "Consumer Awareness Guide" for Win Enterprises to share with our community—a short booklet to help business leaders learn about the consulting industry and how to work with and select a consultant. Obviously, my overachiever traits got the best of me and now we have a full book to share. Terri, thank you for that initial idea, for your guidance in turning this little guide into a book, and for making the process of helping other consultants grow their business a ton of fun.

Jeannette Dardenne—you played such an important role in pulling together the content for the first draft of this back when we were creating a consumer awareness guide. As you read through, see if you can find elements of your work. Thank you for getting the ball rolling!

Kathy Sparrow—a special shout-out to you for helping smooth out the rough edges here. This is the second time you've been a behind-the-scenes "secret weapon" for me on a book. I appreciate your talents and enjoy our chats—you're a joy to work with.

Michael Tasner, our marketing director—you made this book happen now rather than allow it to sit on the back shelf in a perpetual state of 90% complete. Thank you for the push to get it out now because as you so bluntly pointed out: "Pete, it's full of great content that can really help people and it's almost done. Finish it and let's make it a best seller!"

There are plenty of other people along the way who have helped make the content in this book come alive. The countless other consultants that I had the pleasure of getting to know while I was with McKinsey and Company, George Group Consulting, and Accenture all had some influence in this book. The various clients I've served over my career (the first were in 1988!)—I learned something about consulting with every one of our engagements. My fellow executives and business leaders from my time in roles with direct line responsibility—you all helped shape my perspectives about running a business and when consulting support can be part of the solution.

If I didn't call you out specifically, know I appreciate you just the same. Getting a book completed is a major team effort. Thank you to everyone who is part of my team.

Dedication

This book is dedicated to all the business leaders who are struggling to get results and need help.

I understand! I've had the same headaches as you earlier in my career as I had to figure out how to deliver more with less, against tight timelines, amidst supplier crises and customer pressures, all while my family wondered why I was working so many hours.

Know this:

- *You are not alone*
- *Your struggles are unnecessary*
- *There is an easier path to the results you seek (and beyond!)*
- *Working with a consultant can create the fast track to success if you follow the advice in this book*

I want you to excel in your business and not feel stuck any longer. Your frustration is unnecessary once it has done its job to motivate you to take action and tap into the expertise that the right consulting partner can provide for you.

This book is for you as your path away from brute force, struggle, and frustration and toward the systems and processes that deliver breakthrough results that the right consulting partner can bring for you.

Foreword

I have owned as well as operated a variety of businesses during my career including a Speech-Language Pathology clinic, a highly successful home art show company, and I served as president of the largest health care company in the United States.

After my stint in Corporate America, I began coaching business leaders and consulting in companies ranging from small businesses to large fortune 100 companies doing as much as $140 billion in revenue. I have seen firsthand the challenges that companies have, both in the Fortune 500 companies and in the small and medium businesses that fuel our local economies.

Many of these businesses have turned to consultants to help them break through their biggest challenges. And on the surface, this is a pretty good idea, especially when you are stuck and don't know how to solve your problems.

Except, many companies don't understand how to use consultants, or they hire a consultant that just isn't a good fit for them. After spending a lot of money on consulting fees, sometimes after multiple projects, they don't have the results they want to get.

This is a major problem for companies right now because the opportunity, if they actually hired the right consultant to guide them down the path to prosperity, is quite enormous. And, if they did actually have a consultant that is the right fit for them, and understood how to work with a consultant the best way, they would actually achieve business results that exceed what they imagined would be possible.

The key to excelling while working with a consultant to transform your business, crack your problems, navigate your challenges, and lead you to higher revenue and profits is knowing more about the consulting industry and about the consultant you consider hiring. The question is, "just how do you do that?"

The answer is here inside this book.

The author, Pete Winiarski, has a deep background in both consulting and as a business leader. He has been an executive in a Fortune 500 company, and was on the leadership teams of exclusive practices within two of the most prestigious consulting firms. Pete now runs a very successful consulting company, Win Enterprises, LLC.

Pete understands consulting from both sides: from the perspective of the companies who hire consultants, having hired and worked with them himself, and of consultants who deliver the value, having been on the hook as a consulting project leader to deliver millions of dollars of value. With these unique perspectives, he shares what you need to know about the consulting industry and about working with a consultant so you can maximize your ROI when you decide to hire a consultant.

Pete and I also have a special relationship—we both share a passion for helping consultants to deliver the highest value possible while acting in the highest integrity. With this mission in mind, we co-founded the Business Consultant Institute (BCI) together. We have independently observed situations where consultants who are ill equipped or not a fit for some client projects make promises they can't deliver—this hurts the entire consulting industry! We strive to fix this situation by providing the best consultant training and mentoring possible through the BCI.

To make sure that you don't waste your money on the wrong consultant, follow the advice here in this book. Pete lays out everything you need to know to make a great decision that will lead to a huge increase in your profitability and for you to sustain results for the long-term.

Success really is a team sport, and you certainly ought to consider a great consultant as an extended member of your team. The trick is to pick the right one, and this book will guide you to find one who can be your advisor for as long as you continue to have complex problems to solve or huge aspirations for your company.

Pete is genuinely motivated to helping your company navigate the difficult exercise of finding the right consultant for you. Integrity is one of his highest values, and he truly cares for all his business clients of Win Enterprises and all our consultant clients of the Business Consultant Institute.

As you read this book, commit to use the resources that are within these pages. Learn about the mistakes and misconceptions that business leaders have made in the past that have cost them tons of money by unknowingly hiring the wrong consultant. Then, use the guidance here to know how to choose the best consultant for your company.

When you discover from reading this book how to pick the right consultant for your business, and the best way to leverage that consultant to solve your biggest problems and hit your biggest goals, you will be happy about the tons of value and a huge ROI that will come your way.

You will gladly discover that the right consultant can really become your most critical team member.

Terri Levine

Co-founder of the Business Consultant Institute (www.businessconsultant institute.com) and best-selling author of *Elite Business Systems*: *Insider Strategies of Industry Leading Consultants* and of *The Ultimate Game Plan: Power Up Your Consulting Business and Skyrocket Your Revenues.* Founder of the Heart-repreneur® Movement and the best-selling author of *Turbocharge— How to Transform Your Business as a Heart-repreneur®*

Letter to YOU Before We Get Started

Dear Friend,

Congratulations! I want to acknowledge you for obtaining this important book, *Stop Wasting Money on the Wrong Consultant: How to Pick the RIGHT Consultant to Create Huge Profits and Long-term ROI*, as it indicates that you have interest in finding the best consultant for your business. I'm sure that you recognize you can go faster and get better results when you team up with the right consulting resources.

There are many types of consultants out there—in fact, just about anyone can declare him or herself to be a consultant. How do you know if they have the right skills to support you? This book acts like a Consumer Awareness Guide and is designed to help you understand more about consulting and working with a consultant so you can make the best decision to hire the best consultant for your business. We don't want you to make the mistake of hiring the wrong consultant and experience negative ROI and unsustainable results. We want to help you understand how you can make the right choice for your company.

Choosing a consultant can be an important step for you and your company. The right one can save you tons of money and have strategic impact that can position your company for enormous results and long-term success. The wrong consultant can cost you tons of money and create frustration as your team wastes lots of precious time.

Stop Wasting Money on the Wrong Consultant will provide you with the insights you need to make the best decision for you and your company. With the information in this fact-filled book, you'll discover how to avoid costly mistakes, stop wasting money and time, and ensure your lasting success by hiring the best consultant to guide you on your business transformation journey and beyond.

If you have any questions about the information in this guide or about picking a consultant, my team and I are happy to help you and answer your questions. Contact us by phone at +1 860.651.6859 or email us at support@CompleteBusinessTransformation.com. We're dedicated to see our clients succeed by achieving maximum results and wish the same for you.

Sincerely,

Pete Winiarski

Founder and CEO of Win Enterprises, LLC and Creator of the *Win Holistic Transformation Model*™, and Co-Founder of the Business Consultant Institute.

Introduction

You may be wondering why I wrote this book about finding the perfect consultant for you (and suggesting you might be wasting money on the wrong consultant) when I am the CEO of a consulting company. Wouldn't I want business leaders to flock to Win Enterprises without considering other options?

Naturally I would love you for to call our office and say, "I need you to help me!" And, we want you and all our clients to make an informed choice. If Win Enterprises is a great fit to help you with your needs, then of course we want you to call us.

The thing is, there are tons of options and we want you to raise your awareness so you feel confident about whomever you choose as your consulting partner.

Maybe you have hired the "wrong" consultant in the past and experienced frustration in not seeing the ROI you expected. Or, you hired someone who talked a great game but didn't deliver sustainable results because they didn't possess the personal experience in driving the change you were looking for. Maybe the consultant came to your company and implemented a project, left, but didn't teach your team how to sustain those improvements, and eventually you fell back into your old ways. That is majorly frustrating! Having a blueprint is great and an important first step, but actually performing that change effort is something that needs to be carefully orchestrated with you and supported by an experienced consulting partner.

I wrote this book so that you can be informed and know what to look for in the perfect consulting partner so you can get a maximum ROI and see sustainable results.

Before choosing a consultant, you must know what changes you are looking for in your company. A consultant who has held a leadership position and has led these exact changes is ideal. Working with a consultant who is skilled at building your team's internal capabilities will enable you to more easily sustain long-term results with a higher ROI and will quickly pay for themselves.

Look at your consulting partner as an investment, not an expense. They should be able to show you examples of past successes in their own business or positive results they have achieved as a consultant in other businesses they have helped and be confident that you can achieve similar results with their support.

Consider that consulting is a rather confusing industry. Anyone can call himself or herself a consultant so you want to make sure you select a great match for your needs. There are really big consulting companies that have been around for decades and which have dozens of offices in countries all over the world. But, they are quite expensive with fees of as much as $5,000-$10,000 per person per day, and with multiple-person consultant teams you could have a bill of more than half-a-million dollars a month. That said, the return on investment could be enormous. Those firms generally support the larger Fortune 500-size companies who have the financial resources to make investments of that level.

There are also much smaller firms and even one-person consulting companies who might be a better choice for you. It really depends on a multitude of variables, including your current problems and challenges, your aspirations, your urgency for results, your budget or available capital to fund the consultant and the expected speed for you to see financial benefit from the consulting projects.

The level of consulting fee becomes irrelevant if the ROI is large enough or enables the project to pay for itself. Ultimately you will be able to move forward with confidence, engage a consultant that is a great fit for your business, and expect to achieve amazing results beyond anything you could achieve if you were to go alone without support.

The bottom line is a great consulting partner can make a huge positive difference for you and for your company. You can achieve outstanding results with their help, way beyond your wildest dreams and expectations. The problem is if you choose poorly and you select the wrong consulting partner, you will find that your investment turns out to be a waste of money. In fact, you could lose credibility, erode your team's confidence in you, damage your cash flow, and maybe derail your career. Yikes!

I want this book to be a useful guide to help you to make the right decision for you and your business. When you read this book you will become a little bit smarter about the consulting industry and learn what you need to know in your quest to create amazing results in your business with the help of the right consulting partner.

WHO SHOULD READ THIS BOOK?

There are two groups of readers for this book: Business leaders who would decide to hire a consultant, and consultants. Frankly, any business leader who wants to achieve huge results in their business should read through this book just to get a sense of what's possible for you and your business when you work with the right consultant.

It might be that you don't know how to get the results that you want, and it might be that you don't even have an idea of how high up is up. Whether you've hired a consultant to help you in the past, are thinking about hiring a consultant in the future, or are simply curious and want to learn about consulting, this book is for you.

The second group of readers for this book is consultants themselves. As a consultant you should review the tips and advice in this book and see how you stack up and to be aware of what business leaders are thinking as they consider hiring you. You might discover insights that will help you serve clients better.

HOW THIS BOOK IS ORGANIZED

This book is organized into four sections. Section 1, *Everything You Need to Know about the Consulting Industry*, helps you understand this mysterious and complicated industry with the large elite firms, the boutique and specialist firms, and the independent consultants. It helps you unravel what is this consulting industry all about and give you some perspective as you choose the best consultant to partner with on your journey.

Section 2, *How to Work With a Consultant*, talks about the common misconceptions about consultants, the costly mistakes to avoid, and how to select the best consultant for you. Even if you have worked with a consultant in the past you might discover a more broad perspective that expands your awareness of consultants. No consulting company is like any other, so this section will help fill in some of the blanks for you.

Section 3 is called *Common Business Needs for Consulting Support*. Especially in the context of guiding your business transformation, these chapters describe factors unique to those business needs. The chapters in this section include strategy and strategy execution, leadership development, culture shifting, Lean process improvement, and other business needs that you might bump into. Even if you believe your needs for consulting support are currently limited to just a few areas, read all these chapters, as you will gain some important insights.

Section 4 is called, ***The Answer to Your Biggest Question: What Actions Do I Need to Take to Ensure I Hire the Right Consultant?*** Be sure to read this section before you put this book down. Even if you have not yet clearly articulated all your questions and ideas of how to move forward, this section will give you some specific guidance.

By reviewing these four sections you will learn what consulting is all about and ultimately you will learn how to pick the right consultant for you. You will minimize the risk of selecting the wrong consultant and be powered with knowledge to give you confidence as you hire a consultant to support your business transformation.

HOW TO READ THIS BOOK

This book is designed to provide you with quick insights and fast information. I want this to be a useful, at-your-fingertips resource that helps answer your questions with speed and accuracy.

I suggest you skim the whole book cover to cover very quickly. Then, go back and review the table of contents to see which areas you may want to dive into more deeply and read those areas that align with your current issues or questions. Finally, dive into the parts of Section 3 that you're thinking about for your company. Extract the helpful hints in those specific business areas where you may require consulting support. Most importantly, have fun while you read this book!

I suggest you take lots of notes and write directly on the pages here. Underline, circle, highlight, and write in the margins. This is a working resource for you to dig into, not a book to keep in pristine condition on your shelf.

I also recommend you share this book with members of your team as you start a relationship with the consultant you have selected to partner with you for your business transformation initiatives. They will become more comfortable with the idea of some stranger coming into your company and speed up the critical trust-building process.

Beyond learning from the content within this book, I have also put together some bonus resources for you. You can find them at this companion website:

http://www.TheStopWastingMoneyBook.com

Section I
Everything You Need to Know About Consulting

This section really does provide everything you need to know so that you can get started in your quest to find the right consulting partner. Many people don't know a whole lot about consulting. They might have a neighbor who travels each week and is only around on weekends. They know that that person is a consultant, but what does that person do in their job and with their clients? It's really a mystery. They might have been part of a company that hired a consultant in the past, and their view of consultants will be shaped by that specific experience.

This section is short but powerful. It includes some facts and history about where the consulting industry was born and what it has grown into. I'll introduce you to some of the larger or more well known consulting firms. I'll also talk about the caliber of people who become consultants including those buried deep inside those huge consulting firms. I'll then include the different types of engagement models. You might be thinking, "Engagement models? Doesn't a consultant simply show up, help me with my problems, then get on their way?" Well, sort of. The thing is there's lots of ways you can engage an independent consultant or consulting company so it's a good idea to know something about what the options are.

Go ahead and give this section a quick read and see how much your perspective about consulting broadens and opens up.

1

The Consulting Industry and Its Companies

The consulting industry is growing like crazy, as there are tons of companies who are seeking help to turn around their company, solve challenging problems, or take their business to the next level. According to Plunkett Research, Ltd., the market size for consulting services is estimated to be greater than $488 billion world-wide for 2017, with $255 billion in the United States in 2016. Depending on the research, the industry cumulative annual growth rate (CAGR) is running about 4%.

Consultancy.uk reports that Operations Improvement and Financial Advice make up the largest consulting segments, each about 28% of consulting work. IT Consulting is about 20%, and Human Resources and Strategy each about 12% of the total market. North America continues to have the largest use of consultants, running about 40% of the worldwide consulting projects.

Fundamentally, the consulting company provides outside resources to help organizations tackle their challenging problems or to set and achieve exciting aspirational strategies.

Consulting companies often have expertise in functional areas, process expertise, or a specific industry. The larger firms often have expertise across these areas and so you can find an intersection of say Operations Improvement in Pulp and Paper.

Examples of a specific expertise in a functional area include:

- Corporate Strategy
- Operations Improvement
- IT Strategy
- Marketing and Sales
- Financial Concerns, such as advising acquisitions or restructuring debt
- Organizational Design

Examples of specific process expertise include facilitating kaizen events, using "Quality Function Deployment" to guide new product development, or teaching A3 problem solving.

Many consultants have industry expertise such as retail, financial services, consumer packaged goods, or pulp and paper, for example.

Consultants could have a deep technical expertise such as engineering depth, IT programming languages, the ins and outs of social media like Facebook and the Facebook algorithms, website design, search engine optimization and understanding the Google algorithms, or maybe expertise about a certain type of equipment.

There are also consultants who have had a long career building upon their successes over and over again, have now retired, and are entering the consulting world where they help clients by sharing the advice based on their experiences and successes. You might call this been-there-done-that expertise.

The list of different types of experts goes on and on as there are also other deep specialists that could have roles that are totally unique but very useful, For example, I know someone who has deep product development expertise who bills out more than $10,000 per day to deconstruct competitor products and then advise his client on product development improvement ideas to increase performance at a lower cost than the competitors provide. I also know someone who is a purchasing expert for the restaurant industry. There are a plethora of ex-manufacturing Lean process improvement people out there facilitating kaizen events—some with real deep experience and others simply great process facilitators.

CONSULTING HISTORY – NOTABLE TIMELINE

- 1886—Arthur D. Little Inc. was founded
- 1893—Frederick Winslow Taylor, recognized as the father of Scientific Management, began his consulting practice
- 1914—Edwin G. Booz founded Booz Allen Hamilton
- 1926—James O. McKinsey started McKinsey and Company
- 1930s—Consulting focus on finance, strategy, and organization
- 1960s—Strategic Management as a new field with tools and approaches
- 1980—Five firms with greater than 1000 employees
- 1980s—Focus on strategy and organization
- 1990s—More than thirty firms with greater than 1000 employees

HOW TO THINK ABOUT THE CONSULTING INDUSTRY

The industry can be grouped into the "Big Three" strategy firms, medium-sized firms, the consulting divisions of the "Big Four Audit" firms, boutique firms, and independent consultants.

- The "Big Three" strategy consulting firms are McKinsey and Company, Boston Consulting Group, and Bain and Company.
- Medium-sized consulting firms include A. T. Kearney, and could be more than $1billion in revenue, but are smaller than the Big Three.

- The "Big Four Audit" firms are accounting firms who have divisions that offer consulting or advisor services. They include Deloitte, PricewaterhouseCoopers, Ernst & Young, and KPMG.
- Boutique consulting firms are those smaller firms with one or more areas of specialty or expertise. "Boutique" is more about the narrow focus of services than its size.
- Independent consultants are those individuals who offer consulting services, as their expertise is often desirable to businesses. They could be one-person consulting companies or companies with just a few consultants.

The fee level and structure of the consulting support for each type of consulting firm varies greatly. Generally, the larger firms have a higher fee structure because they have a solid reputation for delivering results very quickly. They also have a large number of resources to conduct research and pull data, to create their presentation materials, and to support the core team that is on the ground with clients.

I'm familiar with large teams of more than ten working consultant resources that bill the clients well over a million dollars each month. A small team might be $250,000 to $400,000, and up to $700,000 or more for the most prestigious firms.

Many independent consultants and smaller boutique firms are happy to provide services by just a few resources at a time, and sometimes for less than full-time support. For example, a team of one to three people who support a client for one to three weeks per month is a popular model used by independent consultants.

You will find examples that range from a solo consultant who spends 3-4 days a month with a client all the way up to teams of consultants at each of a dozen client sites around the globe.

NOTABLE LARGE AND MEDIUM CONSULTING FIRMS

The "Big 3" Strategy Consulting firms, McKinsey and Company, Boston Consulting Group, and Bain and Company, are considered the most prestigious consulting firms. Additionally, Accenture is known as the world's largest consulting company. I've also included some information about A.T. Kearney, another well-known consulting firm, and the Big Four Auditors.

Here is some interesting data about each, all pulled from our friendly Wikipedia.com or their direct company websites. While some of the information listed is from a few years back, the order of magnitude is what's really important as you learn about the industry.

McKinsey and Company (2015 and 2016 data)

- Revenue $8.4 billion
- Over 12,000 consultants and nearly 2,000 research and information professionals
- 110 offices in more than 60 countries
- 1,400 plus partners

The Boston Consulting Group (2016 data)

- Revenue $5.6 billion
- 14,000 employees, including 6200 consultants
- 85 offices in 48 different countries.

Bain & Company (2015 and 2016 data)

- Revenue $2.3 billion
- 7,000 employees
- 55 offices in 36 different countries.

Accenture (2016 data)

- Revenue $32.9 billion (Professional Services and Consulting), of which approximately half is Consulting revenue
- 394,000 employees
- Clients in >200 cities in 120 countries

A. T. Kearney (2014 data)

- Revenue $1 billion
- More than 3200 employees: 2300 consultants
- 60 offices in 40 countries

Big Four Auditors

The Big Four Financial Auditor firms are KPMG, Ernst and Young (EY), Deloitte, and PricewaterhouseCoopers (PwC). Each of these firms has some divisions that conduct management consulting services.

EVERYONE IS HIRING CONSULTANTS!

The reason that the consulting industry is booming is because everyone is realizing they can achieve results more quickly with highly qualified help. And, consultants can help businesses in any economy.

In an expanding economy, consultants help you to profitably scale your growth and take advantage of new opportunities. They help you reset your strategies to maximize your benefit as you navigate your growing revenue.

In a contracting economy, consultants help you keep your costs in check while maintaining a leading position in the markets you serve. You might reset your strategies to become more competitive with fundamentals like high quality and service, streamline your operations to become more efficient, or creatively launch a new product or service to capture additional business.

Any way you look at it, the right consultant can help you think through your strategies, develop your capabilities, and execute those strategies well to make the predicted results on paper a reality for you.

Watch the bonus video for this chapter at the companion website for this book:

http://www.TheStopWastingMoneyBook.com

2

Consultants—The People Who Support You

Just like your company is made up of people who have a role to play and do it effectively based on their unique experiences, consultants also have a role to play toward your success.

The resources from the consulting firm you've hired to support you are typically smart, have great analytical skills, and/or have deep expertise that aligns with your company's current problems. You will find that:

- Some consultants are hired directly after college graduation with strong academic backgrounds, but little to no practical experience
- Many consultants have advanced degrees, such as an MBA, Masters in Engineering, or Juris Doctor (law)
- Independent of college degrees, consultants have specific experiences that make them attractive to you
- Consultants can be retired from a career full of rich experiences

The larger firms are full of really smart people even if they don't yet have a lot of experience. The firms make up for these resources' lack of experiences by putting them on large teams where they can learn from their peers. They also have thorough training programs that their consultants go through to sharpen their skills, speed up their learning curve, and standardize their approach to various consulting responsibilities such as leading a team, driving the problem solving process, creating presentations, and communicating with client teams.

Many independent consultants have tremendous depth of experience and expertise, but may lack any formal training in consulting process like problem solving, analytics, presentations, communication, etc.

The best mix seems to be where the individual consultants on the team to support you have a great mix of real world experience and super analytic brainpower, combined with a high emotional intelligence to enable them to navigate the dynamics within your company environment.

Let's face it. You are bringing in a consultant to help drive change in your organization. If your team is resistant to those changes that the consultant is recommending then your results will not improve. In fact, they may degrade even further. It is, therefore, critically important that the consultant resources are capable of communicating to your executive team, your managers, and the front-line employees. They need to be courageous enough to tell it like it is, but to do so in a way that makes everyone comfortable with the message.

During my career, I have encountered too many really smart consultants who lack the communication skills to engage client teams and to build consensus and buy-in to their ideas. They were rarely successful, and this of course impacted the results for the client.

Another important skill that a consulting team member should have is the ability to synthesize tons of data and facts that they have collected or observed. Clients don't need a play-by-play of every single detailed analysis, although that information should be collected as backup for your insights and recommendations. It's the ability to synthesize that information that really makes a consultant so valuable, especially versus the skillsets of typical employees.

Another great consulting resource skill set involves the ability to analyze piles of data very quickly, often using Excel spreadsheet wizardry, which is equivalent to pulling a rabbit out of their hat. To do this effectively and efficiently is important because it enables quick insights and answers for the client.

There are many other impressive skills that your consulting team resources are likely to have. Now that you know what some of these are, you can observe them in action as they work with you and your team.

Watch the bonus video for this chapter at the companion website for this book:

http://www.TheStopWastingMoneyBook.com

3

Types of Engagement Models

The engagement model for a consulting company to work with your business ranges from a single resource who makes periodic "check-in" visits, to a large team of full-time resources over a period of months or even years. Here are some of the popular engagement models you might encounter:

Full-time support over months with teams of multiple consultants.
There can be consultant teams across a variety of functional areas or problems. The cost of this model is the highest, but the return could also be the highest for those businesses that have the financial resources to invest.

Full-time support with a single resource
Here a resource is dedicated to you and does not support other clients. Rather than a full team of people, this model is one individual, working with you and your team, full-time over a period of months. This engagement model may have started with a team of people, but then after an initial burst of knowledge, insights, planning sessions or, data analysis, etc., it might be that your site only requires one resource to manage the follow-up and implementation work.

Part-time support with one or more resources, for 1-3 weeks/month
In this model, the consultant may have other clients they also serve concurrently, or might enjoy a flexible working relationship where they have more

time off. Consulting is a demanding career so this is not an unusual situation. Depending on the scope of work to be handled by your consulting partner, you might still have a team of resources driving multiple streams of work for you.

Short-term visits

Short visits are useful for the consultant to mentor your resources or to facilitate workshops, assign homework, then to depart for a short period before their next visit. This model appears to be more cost effective because your consulting expense will be lower, but it has a heavy burden on you and your team for identifying the focus areas and then for follow-through on implementation. For this reason, there is a higher risk of failure, and a higher probability of subpar results. However, this model works great when the executive team fully owns the project and is driving progress internally. The consultants are really an extension of the executive teams' initiatives in this case.

It's important to realize that there is not one answer for how to best work with and engage a consulting company to support you. Any of these models can be useful to help drive results for you and deliver a huge return on your investment. The important thing is to discover what works best for you, given some other variables. These variables largely are factors within you and your company, as much as they are for the consultant.

VARIABLES TO CONSIDER WHEN DECIDING CONSULTING MODEL

On the consulting side, it's often a function of the skill match, meaning the skills on the consulting team and how well they match up with what you need right now. Beyond skills, it might be a capacity question where you just need more bandwidth, more pairs of hands working the problem, because time is of the essence.

As for factors that depend on you, the client, one decision you need to make is whether the consulting project is a *done-for-you* or *done-with-you* approach.

That question really depends on how important it is to you to have skill transfer from the consultants to you and your resources. In some cases, you're hiring the consultants to come in to share their big brains, come up with the answer to some tough questions, provide you with your list of recommendations, and then they get out of the way for you to make your decision and implement their suggested strategies.

In other cases, you might need a consulting team to execute some projects or major initiatives for you, and you frankly don't have any desire to learn those particular skills or adopt them on to your team. That implies that these particular tasks may be outsourced to your consultant for an extended period of time, but that sometimes is the right decision for you. Outsourcing social media strategies often fall into this category, for example. When implementing big companywide organizational changes, it's often critical to have team engagement and consensus. When that's the case, you want to make sure your consultant is working in a *done-with-you* model. They need to have the skills to build consensus as they are teaching principles and implementing strategies.

Watch the bonus video for this chapter at the companion website for this book:

http://www.TheStopWastingMoneyBook.com

Section II
How to Work with a Consultant

This section, *How to Work with a Consultant*, helps you understand many of the answers to questions that you might not even know you should be asking. In some cases, consultants have a bad rap. Unfortunately, that's probably because of the experience someone had with the wrong consultant for them. That's why it's so important for you to go through and understand the details about the consulting process so that you can pick the perfect consultant for you and be really happy with the return on investment that you get from your consulting partner.

Full of insightful tidbits, this section will help you pick your perfect consulting partner. I talk about why companies turn to consultants in the first place and review signs for you to look for that indicate that you should consider consulting support. There are a number of misconceptions about consulting that I list so that you can have the correct perspective as you interview different consulting firms.

Companies often make costly mistakes when they choose a consultant. I'll discuss how to avoid the mistakes and identify the warning signs that you're not ready to hire a consultant, and also lay out tips for how to make your consulting engagement super successful. I describe some things to think about before you sign the contract with your consulting firm. And lastly, I itemize some of the differences between consulting and coaching, and also consultants versus contractors. Knowing the similarities and differences is important as you make your decision to hire the right consulting partner.

As you consider hiring your next consultant to support you on your business transformation journey, refer to the elements of this section. You may find they help you make a better decision.

4

Why Companies Turn to Consultants

As I've stated before, there are numerous circumstances in which companies may need to hire a consultant. Here are the top fundamental reasons why companies consider consulting support:

1. Inject expertise
2. Add capacity to drive improvement
3. Satisfy your desire for a third-party perspective
4. Motivate your team

INJECT EXPERTISE

There are multiple reasons a client recognizes they need expertise. Say you want to enter a new market space or want to launch new products that use a technology that is new to you. That is a good time to consider a consultant with expertise in that market to give you insights about what the customers really want, or consultants who are familiar with the technology as they have successfully applied it for new product launches. You can see in these two examples how hiring consultants will speed up your learning curve tremendously.

In another example, a consultant to act as your "Lean sensei" will inject the expertise you require to guide your production system design and implementation. Process expertise might be the solution to a number of your company's issues. For example, an expert in the Toyota Production System and in creating Lean operations comes in to act as your Lean sensei, facilitates kaizen events, and guides your production system design and the implementation required through a variety of kaizen-type engagements.

Maybe you need deep maintenance support to improve overall equipment effectiveness. You might bring that consultant or consulting team in because you believe that your equipment can operate more efficiently and produce a higher output than you're getting right now. Your company may be experiencing a challenging problem that you need help to solve. It may be that the consultant has a track record of amazing results and you want that same level of performance in your company.

Perhaps you want to launch a marketing strategy that centers on building a social media presence, yet you don't really understand the algorithms that drive Facebook, LinkedIn, Instagram, or the multitude of other social media platforms. A consultant with the right expertise will save you headaches, time, and money while you try to learn the hard way—by yourself!

In all of these examples, injecting the expertise raises the capability within your company beyond what you had before that consultant came to help you.

ADD CAPACITY TO DRIVE IMPROVEMENT

Once your implementation plan is clear, you will have a ton of work to do. However, consulting support can guide your teams—and even take ownership of specific projects or analyses—so your team is free to work on other projects in parallel.

This is clearly where the *done-for-you* model fits. Often times consultants who are operating in a *done-for-you* engagement model are tackling issues or implementing areas where you and your team simply do not have the interest or capacity to do that work or do drive that improvement.

There's also an interesting phenomenon when an outsider that you trust comes in and joins your company's improvement efforts. They often have much better results in facilitating the different projects that you're taking on as part of your improvement agenda compared to when you have internal resources attempt the same facilitation exercise. Sometimes it's because the internal resources, frankly, are part of the existing culture. The internal company dynamics are at play and your internal resources naturally have to navigate and live within these parameters. The external consultant can come in and break through some of those perceived barriers instantaneously. This is an effectiveness element as well as a capacity element when you bring consultants in from the outside to help you drive your improvement.

Extra capacity could also be required when you don't have the required skills in you company, and you really don't want to bother developing those skills in the new-year. When that is the case, you might just prefer that the consultant takes care of that work for you, at least until you feel you have the time or bandwidth among your resources to take that ownership yourself.

SATISFY YOUR DESIRE FOR A THIRD-PARTY PERSPECTIVE

A reputable third party can help you validate your direction, can provide an assessment, and can facilitate meetings or projects in a way that minimizes the internal biases that risk creating "groupthink"—that team consensus method that accidentally discourages creativity or individual responsibility.

The basic reasons you might want to validate your direction are to prove to YOU if this direction is right, or to help YOUR TEAM understand this direction is right. Let's look at both reasons.

The dynamic that occurs in many situations is that company resources often respond to the guidance from an external consultant better than internal leadership. Leaders bring in an outside expert to gain support for their leadership agenda using the leader's point of view as their starting hypothesis. They dive into the observations and data analyses to prove or disprove the hypothesis. Once the consultant validates the leader's principles, progress tends to accelerate.

The consultant can help build consensus across multiple areas that may have been resisting the ideas from the internal company leadership. They might do this via training programs or by observation and data analysis. Then, it's the same phenomenon where external consultants who are adding capacity to drive improvement are more effective than the internal resources attempting to do the same thing. That effectiveness and the speed of implementation that you are able to experience with the help of your external consultant resource is sometimes so much greater, or at least breaks through barriers that would have prevented you from making any progress at all, that you sometimes wish you hired the consultants in to help you much sooner.

A consultant, as an outsider, can eliminate the biases that exist in most companies when reviewing situations. Your consultant can conduct an assessment and provide their point of view about your real issues, their observations and concerns, your opportunity (often expressed in both operational and financial terms), and the best path forward. Without the external perspective, your company risks being blinded by its team members' limiting pre-existing ideas.

There are many occasions where you have a project or meeting that doesn't live up to its full potential. Maybe your team tends to get stuck in the weeds, can't reach consensus, or doesn't tend to make decisions easily. When this is your pattern, a consultant can play a facilitator role to ensure that your project or meeting stays on track and keeps moving forward.

MOTIVATE YOUR TEAM

There seems to be magic when an external expert shares their thoughts. Your team listens with a different intensity, digests their words, and processes the message they just heard. The strange thing is, even when their thoughts might mirror your perspective, they have more motivational influence. Why? It's that you're familiar to your team while the outside consultant is considered special.

When you want to get your team excited about your direction and motivated to act, or even just to hear what you have to say, bring in a consultant who can reinforce your message. Just as your teenagers might write off your advice because you are their parent (and they believe that they already know more than you do) when someone they respect says essentially the same thing, such as a coach or celebrity, you now have a chance of them following your advice. Recognize this powerful way to use a consultant can move your team to results more quickly.

THE COMBO PLATTER—ALL OF THE ABOVE

It is possible that you bring in a consulting team for all of these reasons. For example, you might want to get help with defining your leadership agenda and ask the consulting team to help you with a diagnostic exercise to determine the level of opportunity that is possible and give you a sense of the different initiatives to launch.

Some of these initiatives may require your team to implement concepts that they are not yet familiar with and certainly don't yet have the expertise, so you continue with consulting support for these projects. Additionally, there are some areas of analysis that you want the consultants to do because it is beyond the capability of your team, or you're afraid if your team takes it on they won't do as thorough a job as the external experts.

Finally, you want to go faster in implementation and your team is at its limit for getting work completed. You add additional consulting resources to give your team a lift.

As you can see, it's easy to continue to engage consulting resources to help you across a wide variety of improvement themes.

Watch the bonus video for this chapter at the companion website for this book:

http://www.TheStopWastingMoneyBook.com

5

Signs You Should Consider Consulting Support

Sometimes companies hire consultants because an executive has a previous relationship with someone in a consulting company. They've worked together before and the consultant has delivered great return on investment and built trust with that client. As people often move from one company to another, the relationships stay strong over time. The executive now at a new company calls his old trusted advisor and shares the new set of situations, challenges and problems that he is faced with in his new role. He has plenty of experience with this consulting resource and knows that consulting support can deliver results much faster than if he tried to slug through it alone.

Another scenario is that an executive simply has worked with consulting companies before and is therefore familiar and comfortable with the consulting process. It may be that they don't hire a known entity, but they still are comfortable with the decision hire in external support because of their positive experiences in the past. Once again, their instincts suggest that getting a consulting resource or team in will get faster results and perhaps more deeply sustainable than if they relied on internal resources. Often speed is one of the bigger drivers to why a company wants to bring in assistance from the outside. Other times it's an executive team's desire to eliminate frustration or pain, but know that they need help to make that happen.

For those of you who have not hired consultants in the past or have not had a positive experience with consultants that you may have used or encountered, here are some other thoughts for you to consider that will help you recognize when you need consulting support to come in and help accelerate your progress.

Here are some signs that you should consider consulting support:

- You are not clear what the **level of opportunity** really is—you know there's opportunity, but you want to confirm the "size of the prize"
- You are not clear what **specific initiatives** you need to launch
- You don't know the **correct sequence** you should implement the list of improvement initiatives
- You want help organizing the **list of strategies** you know will get you huge impact
- You want to **augment your internal initiatives** to **enable faster results**
- You want to coach your team and you **don't have personal capacity** to spend time with each individual
- You realize that you **don't have knowledge or direct experience** on your team to guide you through the details of a particular project
- You want to **build internal expertise** and realize a quick and complete path is with consulting support
- • You **don't have the bandwidth** personally for the level of change leadership required or have capacity on your team to manage all the change that is coming
- You want external expertise to give you input to **validate your assumptions**
- You want consulting resources to **conduct analyses** and help you **create your action agenda**
- You know that **your team will respond to external feedback** better than internal resources—the message will be taken more seriously

Any of the above reasons to engage a consulting company are valid and likely to help you and your team achieve meaningful results more quickly.

Watch the bonus video for this chapter at the companion website for this book:

http://www.TheStopWastingMoneyBook.com

6

Consulting versus Coaching—Both are Critical

Now that you're this far into the document, you have a pretty good idea what consulting is all about. Yet, I'm sometimes asked the questions:

"What about coaching?"

"Should we hire a coach rather than a consultant?" Or,

"I have an executive coach that I'm working with—does that I mean I no longer need consulting support?"

These are valid questions for you to be asking because coaching and consulting are similar. One of the similarities is that these are outside resources that are offering a different perspective to you, as their client, on your various issues and concerns. Both are there to help you, your team, and your company make the improvements required to really excel for the long-term. Think of coaching as a sibling of consulting and know also there are some key differences. Read though the rest of this chapter to appreciate the difference between coaching and consulting.

WHAT IS COACHING?
There are many types of coaches including executive coaches, success coaches, results coaches, business coaches, life coaches, etc. Personal trainers who help you create and monitor your exercise program are coaches, too. Golf coaches

assist you in improving your game and writing coaches guide you through the writing process, whether you're writing a company newsletter or a book.

Each of these coaches has the goal of helping you as an individual to improve your personal results and effectiveness. They help you see your strengths and weaknesses, help you clarify your goals, and get you working on a personal development plan (the kind with positive connotations, not one you are forced to create when you're underperforming!). Your coach may help you to identify and eliminate personal blockages—and distractions that take you off course.

A coach can have a consultative style, which means that they do actually share their opinion. They do so in the context of the coaching relationship, which means that you understand they will sometimes be direct and want them to play this role. They will use their judgment about whether you have the ability to accept what they will say or if they should guide you toward self-discovery.

HOW IS COACHING DIFFERENT FROM CONSULTING?

Coaches usually guide you to *discover* answers rather than tell you what they think your answer should be. A consultant on the other hand is expected to have a point of view and will readily provide you with their thoughts.

A consultant can have a coaching style or play a coaching role during their consulting engagement. Their coaching style will get people to think on their own, much like universities use the Socratic method of teaching. Your consultant may also act as a coach to the different executives, managers, and key resources with whom they interact. As consulting engagements often stretch the limits of the client team members, they find themselves unsure how to behave in these new situations and ask the consultant for guidance.

In a consulting engagement, the consultant may sometimes act as a coach. It is rare that a consultant is also certified as a coach, but some are, and when you find one, know that you have a real gem. If you find that you have personal, mental blocks that need to be removed, it's best to work with an individual who is trained, as some coaches are, to help you rather than a well-meaning consultant.

Both coaching and consulting roles are important for your consulting engagement's success, and are often played by the same person. Some consulting companies have able-bodied coaches on staff that can augment the consulting team's engagement. If you find that the consulting support and process changes are pushing your team members or you beyond your comfort level and you could use coaching, be sure to get the help from a capable coach either from your consulting company's roster or from an independent coach.

Given the large number of unique skills a consultant possesses, it's rare that coach can play a consulting role. For a consultant, however, coaching is a very important role that they will often play depending on the situation.

Watch the bonus video for this chapter at the companion website for this book:

http://www.TheStopWastingMoneyBook.com

7

Contractors versus Consultants— There is a Difference

Just as the question was raised about consultants versus coaches, there is also a question about consultants versus contractors. Let me start by saying, contractors and consultants are not the same thing. However, the language that each company chooses to use may sometimes lead to confusion between these two. The main similarity is that both are outside resources and both really do require a contract in order to have clearly defined roles, deliverables, and a fee structure for the client to pay to receive the value that the contractor or consultant will deliver.

To clarify the similarities and the differences even more, let's get into the discussion about contractors and consultants so that you can appreciate the roles they may play in your company.

WHAT IS A CONTRACTOR?

The interesting dynamic in some companies is that every person who works on site that is not an employee is called a "contractor." This could include temporary labor, a specialized machine repairman, or the external auditors from the accounting firm. Consultants are often lumped in with this group.

An example might be that a company may have a shortage of a key resource, such as engineers or IT programmers, so they get an engineering or IT "contractor" to take on a six- or twelve-month contract to provide an extra pair of hands. To the internal group, they report to a boss and behave on a day-to-day basis as an employee might, yet they are not employees. Contractors work for a different company and are not entitled to any employee benefits. In fact, language in the consultant's contract often designates that the consultant is an external contractor and not an employee.

The contractor is typically an experienced professional who will actually carry out the physical work that needs to be completed. Their service is used by organizations that wish to acquire a given skill set for a period of time, not permanently. Think of them as a professional, temporary labor resource.

CONSULTANTS DELIVER HIGHER VALUE

Consultants are hired more to act as advisors and to lead initiatives versus to "do" an actual job as an employee or contractor might. They may lead training sessions, facilitate workshops, conduct complex analyses, or provide direct support to employee team members who are driving a project.

The thing to recognize is that a consultant is offering a much higher value than a contractor. That said, a consulting company has a contract with the client and so is often labeled a "contractor", and might even have a contractor badge to enter the property. Don't let the name contractor or consultant limit your thoughts of how you're using their expertise. Know what you want and get them to deliver it.

Watch the bonus video for this chapter at the companion website for this book:

http://www.TheStopWastingMoneyBook.com

8

Common Misconceptions about Consulting

If you're a business leader who has already hired consultants in the past and have enjoyed wonderful results and high return on investment as a result of your decision to use consultants, then you are already convinced that hiring your next consultant and consulting team is a good idea to help you with your current set of issues and challenges. Not everyone, however, has worked with consultants before, or some people may have had bad experiences with the consultant they had previously hired.

There are a number of misconceptions about consulting that have been floating around, often times from those who do not have direct experience working with consultants. This fear of the unknown is common and not just for the idea of consultants. Let's face it, we've all heard stories of a company who hired consultants to do some analysis that then led to organizational changes and downsizes that impacted the people who worked in that company and the easiest thing for employees to do is to blame the consultants. It's possible that you have had an experience like this yourself. The reality behind the story is likely to be one where the management of the company found themselves with their backs against the wall and had to make some extremely difficult choices. It might even be that the consultants they brought in helped make a set of decisions that ensured the long-term health of the company as opposed to what might have been even more disastrous if the consultants had not come on board and helped out.

Misconceptions are born because it's a lot easier to blame an outside third party for a series of changes and strategies than it is to look internally (or even to look in the mirror). And, let's face it, not every consultant or consulting firm is perfect for you, which is why I've written this book in the first place. We don't want you to have a bad experience with your consulting partner.

Rather than have you be confused about swirling rumors and misconceptions, I've laid out the most common misconceptions for you here in this chapter. What I suggest you do is read each of these to hear what other people are saying. It might be that some of these misconceptions are held by people on your team and when you announce your decision to bring in a consulting partner to help you, you might experience pushback from people on your team—pushback that is rooted in some of these misconceptions.

Reviewing these misconceptions now will give you a perspective that will enable you to have a more persuasive, fact-based conversation with people who might be pushing back. Avoid letting fear run rampant in your organization. Open your lines of communication and hear what people have to say. If some of their questions and concerns line up with the misconceptions listed in this chapter, then you are already ahead of the game because you will have a response to them.

Misconception 1: Consultants make ridiculously high fees and have no ownership in our results

Consulting fees are based on the value the consultants deliver. If a consulting company didn't deliver results to justify their fees, their reputation would be damaged, they would not get referrals, and they would struggle to pick up new clients. Rather than think about consulting fees as an expense, treat it like an investment with a return on that investment, and be sure you are happy with the projected ROI.

Misconception 2: Consultants come in for this project and leave – they don't have to live here for the long term

The best consultants think of themselves as executives in your company and treat your success as their success. Plus with technology today, it is easy for a consultant to work remotely via phone or web-based communication services (webinars, web chats, etc.) to be available after the engagement ends for follow-up conversation and get your questions answered.

Misconception 3: Consultants are just people with a bunch of school degrees—they don't have real world experience

Some consulting companies, especially the larger ones, do hire consultants right after graduation. These consultants are placed on teams with more senior, experienced consultants who speed up their development and ability to be effective at providing clients huge value. Plus, the formal training and indoctrination into their new consulting company roles is rigorous. In fact, the consultancy would not have considered hiring them if they were not super smart and capable of helping you right away.

Misconception 4: Consultants are just people who failed in the corporate world or in their own business

Consulting is hard work, and if a person failed in his/her own business or in the corporate world they will struggle at consulting. Many consultants choose to break away from the corporate world because they are looking to have more control over their schedules, enjoy helping people, or have officially retired but have been persuaded to join a consulting company because of their expertise.

Misconception 5: Consultants just make up statistics to prove their point

Most of the data consultants refer to is from your systems or process, from your reports, or by their own direct observations. Any data consultants use for comparison comes from publically available sources, other client projects, or the consultant's past experiences. You should indeed challenge them to make sure you understand and agree with their analyses, but it is unlikely that they made up data.

Misconception 6: Consultants don't make recommendations based upon evidence-based outcomes or tested and proven strategies

The opposite is actually true. Consultants have the unique opportunity to work in many different organizations and then draw from those experiences. They are applying proven strategies and frameworks, often modifying them to work in your environment to be sure to move from theoretical to practical.

Misconception 7: The further the consultant had to travel to get to us, the greater their expertise and value

Geography isn't what makes a consultant great. It's their experience, expertise, and ability to apply what they know to help you solve your business problems and implement solutions that sustain over time that creates value. If the consulting company has resources that travel to work with you, it's because they are the best fit for you. Consultants are willing to travel where there is a need for their expertise because they are excited to help solve challenging business problems, but distance travelled is not the most important variable to measure benefit for you. If you're lucky to have the perfect consulting partner for you in your local geography, then seize the moment. If not, freely entertain others.

Misconception 8: Consultants don't lose anything when we fail—we're the ones who have to perform day in and day out

Just like any job, reputation is paramount for consulting companies and their consultants. They rely on repeat business and your referrals. If they are unable to help you achieve great results, their business will directly and indirectly suffer.

Misconception 9: Yeah, but our business is different and since you never worked in our industry you can't help us

There are many similarities across industries, including the processes of how work is completed, the cultural challenges, and leadership behaviors. Consultants bring in a fresh perspective when they come into a new environment. They have the ability to share varied lessons learned from different businesses or industries that indeed apply to help you, too.

Misconception 10: Consultants don't even have to guarantee their work

Many consulting companies guarantee your satisfaction and will do what it takes to make sure you're happy. This often involves adding more resources to your project or extending the team's time. Remember, a consulting company relies on repeat business and referrals so ultimately they know that if you're not happy, their business will not flourish.

Misconception 11: Consultants are just spies and tattle tales for our CEO

CEOs and other business leaders hire consultants for a variety of reasons, including access to an outside expert's point of view. That doesn't make them spies. Consultants know that to be fully effective they have to get buy-in from company leaders and employees. A consultant will often hold progress reviews in order to ensure that everyone feels comfortable and is on board with the changes that they are proposing and leading.

Watch the bonus video for this chapter at the companion website for this book:

http://www.TheStopWastingMoneyBook.com

9

Costly Mistakes When Choosing a Consultant— and How to Avoid These Mistakes

Just as I shared a list of misconceptions that we discussed in the last chapter, there are also some mistakes that companies make when choosing their consulting partner. By raising your awareness about potential risks, you prevent yourself and your team from making these same mistakes.

I think many of the misconceptions in the previous chapter might come from those companies that have experience with consultants but made some of these mistakes listed here. How unfortunate it would be for a company to have made some of these preventable mistakes and then have a sour taste in their mouth about consulting resources. This could possibly lead to a time when they really do have challenges that are beyond their immediate capability to handle, and consulting partners would swiftly help to eliminate the frustrations and clear the path for huge growth and profit trajectories. Leadership in the company might make the choice not to hire consultants but instead to fight the battle themselves. This is a painful way for business leaders to muscle through their challenges and frustrations. It does not need to be that difficult. Every business leader could use an outsider's perspective to help them maintain a clear point of view as they evaluate their options, create their strategies, and execute their plans to get results that they desire. Consulting firms can make that process much easier.

This is what we want for you: a frustration-free, fun, and effortless path to unlimited success in your business for you and for your team. You deserve it! Hiring a consulting partner can help make that come true for you more quickly.

Read through each of these mistakes here. Behind each of the stated mistakes is a short discussion that gives you another perspective so that you can open your eyes and avoid the pain and frustration of poor choices.

Mistake 1: Choosing a consultant solely based on price

Consulting is one of those situations where the axiom "you get what you pay for" often rings true. If you choose your consultant based on price alone, you may be missing out on the experience and skills necessary for your needs, even if you're not aware of what you're missing. Price alone may not offer you the right value for your project because "low price" does not necessarily equal "high ROI."

Do your best to understand what the consulting company will deliver for value and be sure they are a good fit for your business before you evaluate the price.

Mistake 2: Choosing a consultant who can't tie results to a dollar value

You want to see real financial and operational impacts in your business. Your consulting partner must be able to articulate the value they will deliver by implementing their planned initiatives. Ask your consulting partner to estimate the value of the initiatives they are suggesting and probe until you are convinced they know what they are talking about.

Mistake 3: Hiring a consultant who is inflexible in his/her approach and only able to do what they've done before (in situations that might not match yours)

Some consultants have their one great success story (often as an employee executing someone else's strategy). Then, as an independent consultant, they try to repeat what they've done in the past, but don't appreciate all the nuances of your business; therefore, they struggle to get the results they promise. Confirm that your consultant has multiple success stories under their belt, and ask them how they intend to apply business transformation principles in your business.

Mistake 4: Choosing a consultant who is unable to relate to and communicate well at all levels of the organization (CEO to Front Line)

Your consulting team needs to guide people on the front line and advise the executive team. This could be represented by different people on the consulting team, so sometimes a smart consulting resource that works well on the shop floor simply can't communicate succinctly to a CEO, but is augmented by a senior consulting team member who can.

Make sure your partner consulting company speaks your language as an executive, and take them to the area where the work is done to confirm they relate well to hourly workers, too.

Mistake 5: Choosing a consultant who is timid or afraid to give you brutally honest feedback.

Nobody likes to deliver bad news, but you need accurate information. You are hiring your consultant because you are looking for results. Sugar coating the current standing of the organization doesn't help you and could have disastrous results as you step on virtual land mines that could be avoided.

Ask your consultant pointed questions about their opinions and see if they provide direct responses or if they are evasive in their responses.

Mistake 6: Failing to ask for references or case studies.

Having an understanding of the consulting company's past relationships and results from former clients is an important part of choosing the right consultant. Ask them to tell you what strategies they will use to help you, and then ask them if they've done that before. If you want more comfort beyond the answer they provided, ask for one or more references to corroborate their level of expertise.

Mistake 7: Choosing a consultant who doesn't understand how to apply goal-achievement principles to the client's working teams.

There is a science of success that includes the right way to set and achieve goals. Unfortunately, many consultants don't realize there are success strategies to help their teams perform, or they don't understand how to apply these strategies.

Ask your potential consulting company how they utilize goal achievement principles and see if they give you a blank stare or have a cohesive answer.

Mistake 8: Choosing a consultant who cannot work with your culture and leadership styles to achieve the desired results

Without going too deep into it, your culture is basically how your team works together to get things done, and is based in your employees' beliefs, thoughts, and behaviors. Over time, leadership can shape culture. Often times, your change programs will bump up against various types of resistance—from individuals or your larger company culture. Your consulting partner will be ineffective if they don't understand how to shift culture and leadership behaviors.

Ask for examples of culture changes they have led, leadership behaviors they have modified, and how they got results in the face of huge challenges they encountered.

Watch the bonus video for this chapter at the companion website for this book:

http://www.TheStopWastingMoneyBook.com

10

Signing a Contract

This chapter is not legal advice of what elements your contract should contain. Know that it's a good idea to have a contract and to seek the advice of your attorney to help you get it signed and executed.

As part of the process of engaging your consulting partners, it makes sense to protect both you and your consulting partner to have a contract in place. This is a contract between your company and the consulting company that:

- establishes the relationship you have,
- describes the work that you are asking them to complete for you, and
- defines the value exchange, meaning the fee that you're paying for their services, and then it itemizes any other terms and conditions that you want to have in place.

Just like for any other external third-party relationship, a contract is a good idea. With consulting, especially because you may be investing hundreds of thousands of dollars with your consulting partner, a contract is a smart idea for both parties. Let's face it, this is not an example where you are hiring a college kid who lives up the street to come paint your house for you. You probably do not have a contract for that work. You agree to the job, agree on a price, they come smear paint all over your house, once you're happy they give you a bill, and you write them a check. But we're not talking the same order of magnitude of fees or responsibilities in the house-painting example—this is much bigger.

One reason this chapter is part of this book is because, unfortunately, we have seen too many examples where a client and consulting company are progressing with discussions about a particular project and everything looks like it's ready to go, right up until the moment when it comes time to finalize the plans with a contract. That's when something suddenly changes in the mindset of one of the parties. Usually this appears in the form of some underlying fear, and the project doesn't end up starting at all. A contract moves the discussion from theoretical to real for the client, and sometimes they suddenly realize they are simply not ready.

GREAT QUESTIONS TO ASK BEFORE YOU SIGN

You can learn a lot about a consulting company by asking specific questions and listening carefully for the answers—what they say and what they don't say. Here are a list of questions you might consider asking any consultant before hiring them:

- How long have you been in business consulting?
- What other clients have you served that are like us?
- How long have your consultants been on your team?
- Do I get to work with you directly, or am I supported by some of your other consultants?
- What is the expertise of the consultants we will be working with? Can you share their bios?
- What's one of your greatest successes with a client?
- Tell me about a challenging client situation, and what did you learn from the experience?
- How much time should my team expect to invest each week to implement strategies and recommendations?
- What do you put in writing in terms of expectations, results, commitments and terms of engagement?

- If I'm not happy with your consulting, what do we do to resolve it?
- Where did you learn your principles and methods? Who was your mentor?
- Share your past leadership experience. What roles have you played?
- Give us some estimate valuations on the initiatives you are suggesting.
- How will applying your principles help us achieve our strategic goals?
- What are some different process improvement approaches you've used?
- Share some examples of culture changes you have led in the past.
- It would be wonderful to gain some insight on a few leadership behaviors you have modified with past clients.
- Please tell us two large hurdles you have previously encountered in one of your past consulting roles and how you resolved them.
- What question should I be asking that I haven't asked yet?

These questions will help you be confident that the consulting company is the perfect partner for you. They are your advisors and your friends who are going to help you and your team accelerate your progress, conquer the sources of your frustration and solve your problems so that you can grow more profitably. While it's rare that any company asks all these questions, and you might trust your instincts or the recommendation of a trusted friend and decide not to ask any of these questions at all, just having them here as a reference should make you comfortable.

DON'T LET FEAR GET IN THE WAY

Unfortunately, even after finding the right consulting company to partner with and knowing that starting a project is the right thing to do, some business leaders stop short of executing a contract because fear gets in the way. The most common fears include:

- Poor ROI
- Change
- Conflict
- Commitment

Here is a short description of each of the common fears.

Fear of Poor ROI
Nobody wants to pay too much for any service. If you're not convinced of the savings potential, pause and review this with the consultant until you're excited about the possibilities.

Fear of Change
When working with a consultant, you can expect there will be huge changes to processes and job functions. Be sure your consultant will engage your team and plan time for change management activities to help your team acclimate to new ways of doing things.

Fear of Conflict
Your consultants will bring new ideas. What if your team doesn't like or agree with their ideas? What if YOU don't? Will there be a battle of wits? The best thing to do is ask lots of questions and be willing to try new ideas on a limited scale to figure out how to implement what works. If you're using data to guide your discussions and keep emotion out of the equation, conflict will be minimized.

Fear of Commitment
To create sustainable change will require a lot of work over a period of time. Some companies have relationships with their consultants literally for years. If this sounds intimidating, remember that you don't need to commit to long-term, multi-year contracts. Determine the chunk of work that you're willing to sign up for and commit the contract to that much, knowing that you can always add more later.

By the way, even if you, the ultimate decision maker, do not have any of these fears it is possible that members of your team may have these fears present. Don't ignore the possibility. Rather, invite them to participate in an open discussion with you so you can get your team comfortable.

One mistake we've seen is a business leader fully delegates the decision to hire the consultants and gives the team "veto power." Often, a key resource or two pushes back and stops the engagement from starting, either because their ego will not allow them to admit that consulting support can help them, or they have one of these fears that remains unacknowledged.

What often happens is, eventually, you and your team will come around to the idea that the consultant can help you. And then once you do sign the contract and get started, you realize, *"Goodness, I should have done that years ago!"* The content in this chapter can help prevent your regret for not starting soon enough. Review this chapter with an open mind and curiosity as you consider the issues and challenges that you or your team might have as you're in the final stages of launching your consulting project with a signed contract.

Now that you've managed to put your fears behind you, confidently sign the contract and get started right away!

Watch the bonus video for this chapter at the companion website for this book:

http://www.TheStopWastingMoneyBook.com

11

Warning Signs that you're Not
Ready to Hire a Consultant

You're about to make a huge investment that should provide an even bigger ROI. This is exciting, because you will transform your results as you transform your processes, your people, and practically everything you currently do. You will have an amazing experience that has huge positive impact for you, your company, and your team. The results are huge, but so could be your investment in your team's time and effort, which is exactly why you need to be ready for it.

Make sure you're totally ready to support this effort. Sometimes a full-scale engagement isn't the right answer for you today, even though you know you need help. Other times you're certain you and your team is ready. The point is to give thought ahead of time so you can make a conscious decision.

Where as in prior chapters we've talked about misconceptions, mistakes, and fears about working with consultants that could interfere with you getting help that would genuinely provide enormous impact. Here we delve into the legitimate reasons to delay starting your relationship with a consultant. It's important that you are absolutely ready to spring into action when you bring the consultant on board.

The discussion in this chapter is not meant to be a frightening suggestion that you need to wait until everything is perfect before getting started. In fact, if that were the case, you might never start. Waiting until everything is perfect is rarely a good idea. However, with that said, there are some times that the answer might be to delay the start of your project, and those times are usually because there's some critical element that's not quite right, and by not having that critical element in place your project is at risk of not achieving its full potential or you achieving the maximum ROI that is possible with your consulting partners.

To help you evaluate if you are in that situation, we've come up with a list of different warning signs for you to review and reflect upon. Here's the caveat: this list of warning signs is not meant to scare you out of working with consultants. Rather, it's to make sure that you've given some deliberate thought to these elements. Making the decision to hire consultants is a big deal. We want you to be successful, and we want the consultants that you choose to work with to also be successful. It's a win-win relationship. If you hire consultants before you are ready to line up your teams to maximize the success of the projects that your consultants will guide you through, then it may not be the right time to start the consulting project. Read these typical warning signs to see if you are experiencing any of these at this moment. If not, you're in the clear. Go forth full speed ahead!

WARNING SIGNS
Here are example signs that now might not be the best time for a full transformation guided by a consulting partner.

You Were Acquired
Your company was just bought by a private equity company, and you don't know if the new CEO will support your initiatives. It's best to make sure that your initiatives are safely part of the new strategy before committing to big contracts, or at least build in a contingency to enable you to cancel with notice and minimal penalties should you get started but then discover a direction change cancels your funding.

You Lost Major Customers

You just lost some key customers and your revenue dropped by 20%. Unless the consulting project is about to help you liberate costs beyond that same 20% decrease in revenue, and you don't otherwise know how to do that, you might delay the start until you're able to see a path to recover at least some revenue.

You Lost a Key Employee

The key team member who directly owns the area your consulting partner is to support unexpectedly quits. You have a choice to go forward because you need progress now, or you delay until you hire their replacement. Often the better answer is to keep marching full steam ahead, but at least make a deliberate decision.

You Have Multiple, Major Initiatives

You have some HUGE initiatives that are taking everyone's attention right now. For example, one client recently delayed the major support that we were discussing because they were moving facilities. The equipment moves took a lot longer than they predicted, so our support was limited to a lighter-touch model until they were completely moved into the new location and able to then entertain a bigger engagement.

You Have Issues With Your Team

Team issues come in many forms. For example, you might find your current team is not capable of delivering the results you want, and you need to replace some key people on your team. Perhaps you have influential team members who are resistant to change and you need to modify their beliefs about what is possible. It is also possible that your team is overstaffed and you want to downsize before you have a consultant come in so they don't get blamed for the job loss. You might also have a team that is completely overwhelmed and believes that they cannot currently take on any other work.

By the way, if your team is overwhelmed, a consultant can actually help to streamline processes, understand waste and non-value adding steps, and eliminate complexity. That may be the perfect time to bring in a consultant.

Your Budget Is Stretched

You didn't budget for consulting support and don't know how you'll pay for it because you're thinking of consulting as an expense, not an investment with an ROI. This one is easy to address once you shift your thinking to understand the ROI. Dive into the next chapter if you bump into this situation.

MAKE A CONSCIOUS, DELIBERATE DECISION

These above considerations are not always roadblocks that will prevent you from starting a consulting project. They are important considerations for you so that you make a conscious, deliberate decision. It's best to have a realistic perspective about the level of commitment that you are about to make so that you can make the best choice. If you decide to delay, use caution about delaying indefinitely because you may accidentally find yourself down the road with a missed opportunity to drive results much higher than that your team actually achieved. Define some criteria to trigger a review to evaluate if now is the time for consulting support.

Remember, you don't necessarily need to have already budgeted for consulting fees if the ROI can deliver savings in a reasonable time period. If you can get permission to see the ROI by the end of this fiscal year, you would be better going full steam ahead to get the savings now versus waiting until the next budget cycle begins.

If you decide to start now despite your challenging situations, include your consulting partner in discussions about your reservations and why you still chose to move forward. They will better appreciate the dynamics in your business and may have ideas that can help you.

Watch the bonus video for this chapter at the companion website for this book:

http://www.TheStopWastingMoneyBook.com

12

The Importance of ROI versus Price

At this stage in the book, if you read all of the prior chapters then I am sure you will have a really solid perspective of the need to make decisions about your consulting partner based on the return on investment (ROI) that they will provide for your hiring them.

Let's face it, you're about to invest tens of thousands, hundreds of thousands or even millions of dollars on consulting services depending on the magnitude of the projects you are having your consultants support you with. In my experience, consultants deliver literally millions of dollars of value in a relativity short period of time. With all the variables that would lead to a high return on investment that we described in this book you are positioned to maximize that return on investment. Even with all of this in mind it's still critically important for you to always be thinking about return on investment, which is why we included this short chapter to reemphasize these critical points.

If miraculously you were to find consulting firms that were identical in every single way then, and only then, would it make sense for the lower price to come into play as a factor for you to decide on which consulting resource you were to hire. The reality is, however, that no two consulting firms are identical. I say that even in those examples where the work that you are asking the consultant to perform or the problem that you are asking them to solve may seem rather narrowly focused. It's often the invisible intangibles that make the difference. It's the "what else" do you get for having hired the consultant on that makes the difference from one consulting firm to the next, even when on paper it may not seem that different. Go out of your way to ask the deeper and more challenging questions of each of the consulting firms so you know exactly what it is you're getting.

We have seen examples where someone hired a consultant based on a lower fee level only to later be disappointed at the lack of depth that the consultant really had in their abilities to solve the client's problems. In other examples, the client was happy only until later discussions revealed that another consultant would have delivered a lot more, both tangibly and intangibly.

It is critical that you make your decision about which consultant to use based on their fit with your business and the projected return on investment, and do not base your decision on price alone.

When selecting a consultant that fits your business needs, price will inevitably play a big role in your decision, but should not be your only deciding factor. Consider these important points:

Consulting Services Are Not a Commodity

Purchasing Managers may want to get involved with selecting the consultant because some treat EVERYTHING as a commodity – this is dangerous because they will often go after the lowest price and attempt to negotiate the way they do office supplies. This will introduce huge risk that the consultant they drive you to select might not be able to deliver any more than the bare minimum results. It's not about meeting minimum specifications in a statement of work but rather appreciating how the consultant will add value for you.

There Are Differences In Who You Work With and What They Offer

Know the difference and understand that the lowest price resources may not be the best for you to hire. You might find that you get way more ROI from a resource that is at a higher fee level. This is a function of both value and the level of your investment in fees, and value extends to intangible value along with hard dollars your consulting partner creates for you. Do what you can to estimate value so you can figure out the best ROI.

Understand Why a Consultant Prices His Or Her Services the Way They Do, and What You Get Beyond the Bare Minimum

Some consultants will deliver exactly what you request, and no more for a specific fee level. Many consultants are willing to make at least a portion of their fees contingent on results, and others set their fee as a percent of the value they create, either as new revenue or as cost savings. You might be happy to pay more for a consultant's project by spreading payment over a longer period of time. You might even come up with some other creative pay arrangements that would make a consultant the right choice for you provided you are confident in their ability to deliver results for you.

Make Sure Their Expertise Fits with What You're Trying to Accomplish, and See That They Have Expertise and Bandwidth to Support You in Other Areas Beyond Your Initial Request

You will likely discover you have huge opportunities in areas beyond your initial request, and the best consulting company to help you is the one that gets to thoroughly know your business so they can easily be effective on projects in other areas for you. A consultant who has a super narrow skill set may be limited to helping you with only their current project scope, causing you to recruit and hire a different consultant for the next area.

Consider How They Will Ensure Lasting Results

You want your consulting partner to check in after the initial engagement is complete to confirm the impact of their work is still in place—and if not, to know they can help solve the problems that are preventing you from achieving results.

Look at Their Track Record of Past Successes at Other Companies and Get a Sense of the ROI Level You Can Expect

You can simply ask the consultant to share case studies and even introduce you to their past clients so you can check in about details from a client's perspective. Dig to understand direct value in terms of dollars saved or created as well as intangibles such as the type of interactions with your team and the general impression they left on your company.

Watch the bonus video for this chapter at the companion website for this book:

http://www.TheStopWastingMoneyBook.com

13

Maximize ROI Principles—How to Make Your Consulting Engagement Super Successful

Congratulations! You've decided to hire your consulting partner to help you with your business transformation. You've navigated all of the fears, considerations, and roadblocks that could have delayed your project. You've signed a contract and now you're ready to get started. You probably had some discussion with your team and with your consulting partner about the value that they would deliver versus the fee that you are paying your consultants to deliver that value. This is a return on investment decision. Just like any other major project work you take on, there is some variability with the actual value that you will get from your consulting project. What we want you to do is have all of the mechanisms in place so that you can maximize the value that you receive which in turn maximizes the return on your investment.

Whenever you invest a significant amount of money with the aim at getting a high return on your investment, there are some things that you can do to maximize the ROI. For example, think of investing in a new enterprise software solution. You would be diligent in planning, execution, follow-up with review meetings, etc. This is all true for consulting, too.

You can impact your consulting engagement in such a way to get the most out of your experience with the consultants and boost your ROI. Here are some ideas for you to consider that will help you achieve maximum returns:

Maximize Consulting ROI principle 1: *Have clear goals and deliverables*

Everyone benefits from clear expectations, especially when they are in writing. Taking time up front to define and communicate clear goals and deliverables will prevent finger pointing later if things don't go as planned, and will provide a framework for you to quickly get the project back on track. Of course, having goals and deliverables described well in your contract is a solid start. Additionally, for each separate work stream, project, analysis, and meeting, it will help to state the goals and deliverables right at the beginning. When you do, the consulting team will line up their work to make sure they are delivering what's expected.

Maximize Consulting ROI principle 2: *Hold regular progress reviews*

With clear expectations, you will want to check with the consulting team frequently to make sure they are on track. A progress review rhythm where you have review meetings scheduled on your calendar will help make sure that you have check-points within the engagement. If things are not going according to plan, you have an opportunity to make some adjustments and gain alignment quickly before things get out of hand. The frequency of progress reviews depends on the planned duration of your engagement. For example, in a 1-2 week project, I like to have a short check-in each day for 30 minutes, with a kick-off on the first day and a final review on the last day. For projects that run many months, a progress review every 3-4 weeks works well. Depending on the type of engagement, you could have your company team members do a lot of the presenting, which gives the spotlight to employees who you are developing under the guidance of your consultant—give them public recognition for their taking ownership for elements of the project.

Maximize Consulting ROI principle 3: *Ask lots of questions*

Your best tool with consultants is to ask tons of questions. Ask them what they are doing, why they are doing it, etc. Make sure you understand the plan to deliver the project goals and if the project is on track or not, and then what is next. Check in to see if your team is supporting them and doing what is asked of them and see what the consultant might require from you. Review their analyses and output, and ask questions to challenge their thinking and to help you and your team learn from them. Have this discussion in a positive and engaging way, as you truly are partners toward creating huge improvement for your team and company.

Maximize consulting ROI principle 4: *Ensure your team has a positive mindset*

You want to have your team excited about working with the consultants, not be resistant or threatened by them. Help your team develop this mindset so everyone is working together. Your team will follow your lead on this. If they see your high level of enthusiasm for the consulting project and the consultants working with you then they will be more apt to follow suit. That said, each team member and employee has their own past experiences and may feel threatened, not because the threat is real, but because of something that happened years earlier at a different company. You can mitigate this by meeting with your team, sharing your clear expectations and inviting open dialogue. You're investing a lot of money in the consultants and when your team openly collaborates your results will improve the fastest.

Maximize Consulting ROI principle 5: *Spend as much time with the consultants as you can*

Beyond the progress review meetings you have scheduled, go out of your way to interact with the consultants as often as you can. Sit in during meetings and workshops they are running, or informally pop into their team's workspace. Ask questions and engage them in dialogue. Learn as much as you can from them, as it will deepen your understanding of your business and will make you more effective. You might also join the consultants for dinner periodically in a relaxed atmosphere outside your office so you can get to know each other as people and form a tighter relationship. It also enables you to have unconstrained discussions about the project or about other challenges you are experiencing. You will learn how each other think, which will then make other interactions more efficient.

Maximize Consulting ROI principle 6: *Assign the consultants a liaison*

Assign someone from your team to be the direct point of contact for the consulting team. The liaison can help with logistics like scheduling meetings, getting supplies, finding the right people to talk to, etc. This will make the consultants more efficient and keep them from spending too much time on logistical items and more time adding value for you. Additionally, the liaison can help the consultants navigate your culture and get things done more efficiently within your cultural dynamics. They will know that Alex Jones likes to meet in his office while Sally Smith is so busy you might have to catch her before her first meeting. The liaison might also know about existing dynamics, such as Joe Black was Jackie White's old boss and they didn't get along well, or that Kathy Appleton is the CEO's daughter-in-law. Every company has stories like these that could be disruptive to the project's dynamics if not handled along with the plans to execute.

Maximize Consulting ROI principle 7: *Take a long-term and big-picture view*

It is very likely that hiring the consultant is just the beginning of a long relationship that you will develop with them, even if your initial project is just a few weeks. Allow them to be your trusted advisors that continue taking you and your team to new heights. Expect that they will deliver great ROI for your current project and use all the principles listed here to make sure you enjoy huge impact. While your consulting partner is supporting this current project, constantly evaluate them—how they work with your team to deliver great results. Imagine different scenarios where you might ask them for support to solve other problems and help you with your next challenge. Part of the benefit you receive in your current project is that the consultant gets to know your company's issues and aspirations, your people and culture. If you have other areas where you could use help, consider having your consulting partner join for additional projects. It's a much higher leverage of their resources for you.

To help you understand how important it is to put as many of these principles in place, let me illustrate what the opposite would look like. You would achieve poor results and a minimal ROI if you did not bother to define clear goals or deliverables, did not hold progress reviews, did not ask any questions, allowed your team to have a negative mindset about the consultants, didn't bother to spend any time with them, let the consultant take care of their own scheduling and logistics, and take a super short-term view of your relationship. When you see it this way it seems pretty silly to ignore these principles.

Here's a bonus principle that we strongly believe in for everything we do.

Bonus Maximize Consulting ROI principle: *Have fun!*
Everything that you do should be fun. Transforming your company should be fun, and so should how you do it. Have fun with your consulting partner, your teams, and in all that you do.

Watch the bonus video for this chapter at the companion website for this book:

http://www.TheStopWastingMoneyBook.com

Section III
Common Business Needs
for Consulting Support

This section is all about common business needs for consulting support as part of your business transformation. There are many areas of any business that are critical to get right for you to enjoy long-term success, sustainable growth, and high profit and cash flow. This is true for small businesses in every community across the world as much as it is for giant international corporations.

The chapters in this section are significantly longer than those in Sections I and II because I reveal a lot of detail in each of these areas for you. I want these chapters to be resources that you come back to over time.

The first area I share some insightful thoughts about is *Strategy and Strategy Execution*. The next area is *Leadership and Leadership Development*. Third is *Culture Shifting*. Fourth is *Lean Thinking and Lean Process Improvement*. I also give some insight to some other common business needs where consulting support can help, such as Teamwork, Organization Structure, Problem Solving, IT Systems, and pursuing The Shingo Prize and Other Award Programs that recognize business transformation success.

As you consider different elements of your business transformation, this is a great section for you to skim through and then pick the detailed area where you are currently dissatisfied or considering gaining some support from a consulting partner to digest more deeply. Then you can decide if now is a good time for you to engage a consultant to help you get the results you want.

Learn what you can about these areas so that you can select the best consulting partner and maximize your ROI!

14

Strategy and *Strategy Execution* Consulting Engagements

trategy and strategy execution are important factors in any business. Strategy is essentially coming up with a long-term view of where you want to go and then making sure that you have reasonable plans to get you there. Strategy Execution is about how well you implement those plans—the actions that will transform your vision into a reality. We consultants often talk about strategic goals as the milestones that you set for your business out a few years, commonly 3-5 years. Your strategic goals should align with your company's vision and force you to stretch outside your comfort zone.

This is a good point to introduce the alignment concept to make sure that you have clarity and alignment in your company about what is important in the first place. Typically, we talk about purpose, vision, mission, and goals all requiring alignment to avoid confusing your organization—meaning your executive team, your business leaders, and all your employees have clarity of why you are in business in the first place, where you're going, how you plan to get there, and how you know if you're on track.

Let me share some quick definitions here:

- **Purpose** is *why* you are in business.
- **Vision** is *what your world looks like* when you are achieving your company's purpose.

- **Mission** is what your company is on this planet to do and *how* it achieves its purpose.
- **Goals** refer to those strategic goals that align with your purpose, vision, and mission in such a way that you can assure that by achieving them you will continually make progress towards living your company's purpose and vision while delivering your mission.

Now that you have goals, the next step is to determine the strategies to achieve those goals. Once you have your strategies defined, you and your team need to execute those strategies so that your company can actually reach those goals. If this sounds like a mouth full and a lot to pull together it's because it is!

This is all critically important to have clearly articulated in your company. It can be confusing for those business leaders who are lacking some of these elements or whose team has struggled to achieve the results that they laid out on paper. Executing the strategy is often a challenge. It's one thing to have a beautifully written and documented strategy in a three-ring binder. It's another thing to actually realize what you set forth and defined in your strategy document.

Many companies have a strategy process, especially those publically traded businesses where redefining the strategy on an annual basis is part of their annual business cycle. Once the strategy is approved by the board of directors, and the executive team and the associated budgets to support that business plan are approved, the team then needs to execute what it has described.

Many of these strategy documents are based upon market conditions and define at some level the game the company is playing and what must be done to win that game. Some considerations are: the products and services that your company provides; the geographies you choose to do business in; and an analysis of your competitors and what your competitors are doing within their similar businesses. Additionally, there might be discussion about technology advances. Certainly, you can include in your comprehensive strategy document an itemization of where your risks are and what you would do to mitigate those risks. There is also usually some itemization of where you are the strong market leader and what you can do to maintain that leadership position.

With all of this in mind, your task then is to create a set of milestones where you predict where you will be five years out, three years out, and one year out. For example, now that you have your strategy and your goals itemized, it's time to convert that well-thought out document into specific action plans and strategies that will create the progress and deliver the results that are itemized in the strategy. That is where strategy execution comes into the mix.

Whether you are an international corporation with business in countries around the world or you are small local business that serves your local community, it's one thing to have goals that you wish to achieve some day, it's another thing to make those goals a reality. There are processes to put in place to engage your team members, hold people accountable, and enjoy the fruit of your individual and your team's labor as you achieve these exciting results. The problem is many companies do not deliver anything close to what their strategy documents declare. That's why strategy execution processes are so important.

With that overview of strategy and strategy execution in mind, let's review how strategy consulting began in the first place.

THE RISE OF STRATEGY CONSULTING

Many of the larger more prestigious consulting firms that we mentioned earlier in this book have made their name in helping large businesses with their strategies. Firms like McKinsey & Company, Boston Consulting Group, or Bain & Company are known as the "go to" choices for Fortune 100-sized companies because they have their own research staff to add to their big brain consultants. They are equipped to analyze and synthesize your situation with market analysis, product analysis, pricing analysis, operations analysis, technologies analysis, economic analysis, and host of other potential analysis that fit into their equations, algorithms and processes to help you to answer what business you should be in and compare to what business you are in today so that you can define your strategies to keep your company relevant and thriving.

Many of the strategy consulting engagements end after your consultants did the work then give you a "high five" as they leave you with your newly documented strategy. The implementation, however, is up to you. When you're about to make some strategic choices, you want confidence with data-backed input to help you know what your options are and to help you and your team make those difficult decisions. You'll want an assessment of all of the trends, both external macro-economic trends and your internal micro economic trends.

While a company will invest hundreds of thousands of dollars or even millions of dollars for this sort of consulting, it pays back because we are talking about a long-term future of your business where you are thriving. Consulting engagements of this magnitude create value totaling multiple millions of dollars.

Of course, you have to execute the strategy well to realize your potential. This is why strategy execution consulting has come in to the forefront in recent years. Let's read more about why in this next section.

STRATEGY EXECUTION

Strategy Execution is a rather broad umbrella defining any consulting support that has to do with implementing processes or principles and for projects that have anything to do with delivering results to achieve your strategic goals.

However, specifically in this context, we're talking about processes that are deliberately designed to take your strategy, usually in the format of your strategy document, then define and develop specific actions, projects, and initiatives that are required to execute the strategy and achieve those strategic goals.

This will include metrics with targets and individual owners of those metrics who are held accountable for achievement of results. Each of those metrics are defined to support those initiatives and themes that will then deliver the strategy.

There are numerous methodologies and processes that have been created in recent years to help take theses long-term visions and well-written strategy documents, and turn them into the detailed planning and execution required to actually achieve those strategic goals. One of the more popular methodologies is called Hoshin Kanri. This process originated with Bridgestone Tire in Japan back in the 1950s. It has since expanded to include multiple versions that companies have used and have personalized along the way. Today, there are multiple names for the different versions of this process such as Policy Deployment, Strategy Deployment, and Strategic Goal Deployment™ just to name a few. At Win Enterprises, LLC, we have created our own priority methodology we call SEE™, which incorporates Strategic Goal Deployment™, Engagement, and then Execution processes.

STRATEGY AND STRATEGY EXECUTION— SIMILARITIES AND DIFFERENCES

Clearly, you can see that both creating and executing your strategy are important. It doesn't help if you have a wonderfully documented strategy that sits in a binder but then does not become a reality. So one might argue strategy execution is more important than the strategy itself. On the other hand, if you're striving to get away from "business as usual" and recognize that there are competitive pressures that you need to address, you may need to change your business model and how you approach the market place. In this instance, creating and documenting your strategy may indeed be most important exercise for you.

Today, some strategy consulting work includes the strategy execution piece and some strategy execution includes the consulting team to help you create your strategy that drives you in the first place. It really depends on your situation and how your consulting partner typically operates. Be sure to ask questions to confirm the scope of your engagement so that there are not any misunderstandings that leave you dissatisfied.

One thing to know about strategy consulting is that while the return on investment could be enormous (and may save your company from extinction or enable it to take a market leadership position for the long-term) the ROI may not be immediate. However, some of the strategy execution consulting work will in fact deliver results very quickly which will make you and your finance leader very happy.

Let's look at what I mean by this:

Say you invest in a consulting team of resources who dive into the market's micro- and macro-economic details. The team conducts some tremendous analysis that convinces you to redo your network of production and distribution facilities, that you need to open a market in a new geography, or that you might need to close or sell off a significant portion of your existing business. This sizable investment in consulting fees to develop that particular strategy gets you up to the starting line for any execution work.

A better way to think about the return on investment for the strategy consulting work is that with new strategic insights you may discover that your company is at risk but also what to do about it to prevent competitors from passing you by. And that includes new competitors who rise to the scene seemingly overnight. That is one of the biggest challenges that companies who have been around for decades are faced with today. What seemed like good business 10-20 years ago might now be antiquated as a new economy start-up comes out of nowhere and disrupts your industry, much like Uber and Lyft have done to all of the taxi services around the world.

If a consultant can help you recognize that your industry's equivalent of Uber is poised to attack, you can make changes to defend yourself or even to get ahead of the curve and launch your own version of Uber for your industry before anyone else gets there. Then you might very well have saved your company from a huge disaster. This is the real value of strategy consulting work. It's not measured in short-term viewpoints of return on investment, but rather a long-term viewpoint that differentiates between those that barely survive and those who learn to thrive in the ever-changing market we all live in.

Strategy execution, on the other hand, is about getting results along the way so that you can get the pieces in place and achieve your strategic goals. Some of what strategy execution requires is putting some building blocks in place that might include new capabilities that you don't currently have in your organization. That is an investment that will take a little longer to pay back. Other elements of strategy execution will be more immediate in putting dollars to you bottom line.

For example, if the strategy includes a network optimization where you consolidated production facilities or distribution sites, you're not going to do this feverously. It will take some time to methodically analyze what sites to close and which will absorb the additional volume, all while serving your customer without any hiccups. The analyses and execution required will lead to a more efficient network that is able to service costumers at a lower cost and higher delivery. You can expect that lower cost to be measured in millions in most cases.

For many businesses, strategy execution is really about goal-achievement principles applied to your businesses. Elements of keeping the team focused on the most important activities, creating action plans that detail out exactly what work needs to be accomplished, and defining who's accountable for what pieces of the work are all elements that you would see in large and small companies. It's clear, however, that these elements are very important in smaller businesses that might not have to make decisions such as network optimization.

Now that you have a sense of how strategy and strategy execution engagement fit together, let's talk about why you should consider strategy or strategy execution consulting support.

POTENTIAL ELEMENTS OF A *STRATEGY* ENGAGEMENT

Saying that you need help with your strategy leaves a lot of room for interpretation. Here is a quick summary of some of the elements that might be part of the engagement when you hire your consulting partner to help you with these areas.

Deep Review of Your Financials

Frankly, any consultant in any engagement will take a look at your financial statements to make sure that they discover the most important levers in your business and can also tie back any process improvements to calculate financial value. In a strategy engagement, it's likely that you will have your consulting partner conduct a rather in-depth review and analysis of your financial statements. It's important to know where you are right now—and it's important to have this basis in mind as different potential strategies are discussed. Each strategy needs to have the financial impact laid out so that it's clear what you will gain from implementing these different strategies.

Deep Review of Your Market Position

A strategy engagement could also look at where your product and service offerings are in relation to other players in the market. It's important to have a sense of whether or not you are in the number one or number two position, or if you are deeper in the pack. Further, for those where you are not number one, it's worth knowing whether or not you have some potential to make up ground, take that number one position, or if some of your deeper products and service offerings should be trimmed and you refocus on the winners.

Analysis of Market Trends

It's a good idea to know what's going on in your current market and to anticipate what might be happening in the next couple of years. The last thing you want to do is miss a solid opportunity by falling asleep and not seeing these market opportunities coming at you.

Review of Advancing Technologies

As technology changes around you, these changes will certainly have implications for your products or service offerings. Remember when your car had a carburetor? Just as new automobile technology led to fuel injection and eliminated the need for a carburetor, you might have opportunities to apply new technologies in what you do and seriously upgrade what it is you offer. This of course would also put your competitors in a position where they are chasing you as the core leader.

Recommendations about Products and Services

From all of the above, you can expect a set of recommendations about what products and services you might phase out, start up, or acquire. If there is an excellent opportunity, given the market trend, you might want to launch a new product idea or to apply a new technology to give you an advantage in the same market space you already serve. This becomes a dialogue that you can expect within your strategy engagement. Also, if you have a lot of complexity in your processes or in your products and service offerings, you might receive recommendations to eliminate some of that complexity which will then provide cost advantages for your overall business strategies.

Recommendations about Geographies

The analyses that your consulting partner will perform in a strategy engagement might also lead to suggestions about what geographies might make sense as you consider expanding your reach. For example, a regional business might have the opportunity to roll out a product on a larger level with the proper distribution channels across the country. Some businesses that are already nationally based might have opportunities to go international.

Recommendations about Capabilities to Develop

Strategy is also about being able to win the game. Just like a sport analogy where you want more depth in certain key positions or want a superstar to lead you to the championship, you might need to acquire some skills that you don't currently have on your team. These skills can be in the form of creating a new department or division, or might be as simple as hiring a key player with deep skills that give you some capability that you do not possess. Capability could also be acquiring a new technology, or applying technology in a way that you are not currently.

You need the right skills in your team and within your organization to implement the right strategies. A consultant providing you with possibilities in your strategy engagement can do just that. That's where a strategy execution engagement comes in.

POTENTIAL ELEMENTS OF *STRATEGY EXECUTION* ENGAGEMENT

A Strategy Execution engagement is also rather wide open—supporting any initiatives that help make your strategy a reality. In what I outline here, I am specific about a governance process that ensures your company stays focused and on track toward executing your strategy. Here are the common elements your consulting partner could help you achieve in this engagement.

Converting Your Strategy into Strategic Goals

Once your strategy is defined, it's important to articulate those strategic goals that you set your for your business. Long-term goals are important, but it's also vital to convert the longer-term goals into your goals for the next year. This will enable your team to have clarity about what they are working on right now.

Cascading the Goals through Your Organization

The idea here is to make sure that the leaders of different functional areas and teams in your organization know which goals they are directly supporting. There are different consultants will use to help you accomplish your strategic goals. The critical factor is that your teams have the focus required to make an impact.

Defining Specific Initiatives

This part of a strategy execution engagement will help make it clear what initiatives and major themes are the most important and will have the impact you need to achieve the goals you have set. With the initiatives you define, be sure to indicate who owns those initiatives and how successful implementation of those initiatives is measured.

Creating a Rhythm of Progress Review Sessions

Your consulting partner will help mentor your leadership team to make sure that they are asking the correct questions to those leaders who own specific initiatives and the corresponding metrics and targets. The rhythm of these progress review sessions might be different from company to company, but it is important to establish what that rhythm will be for your business. These progress reviews are critically paramount for you to confirm that you are on track and also to teach your team what is expected of them.

Guiding Problem Solving

It is rare that all of your plans will execute on time without any challenges. It is also rare that the plans you develop will deliver the exact results you expect. Because of this it is crucial to teach problem solving techniques to help your team learn what they must do to respond to any gaps in expected progress.

Mentoring Business Leaders and "Accountable Metric Owners"

Your consulting partner is not just there to aid in analyses and provide encouragement. When they finish the engagement, they want to make sure that you and your team are capable of continuing to drive strategy execution with the same level of rigor and enthusiasm as when they were there helping you directly. They will support and model the behaviors, the types of questions to ask, and the detail dialogue that you and your business leaders should expect to be asking of your teams. Additionally, the consultants should teach those who we call "Accountable Metric Owners"—your team members who own a specific metric and are accountable for hitting the targets—to take on full responsibility for the results of their initiatives and need to learn how to respond to these questions to anticipate them in the first place. This mentoring is critical for your long-term success.

COSTLY MISTAKES WHEN CHOOSING A STRATEGY OR STRATEGY EXECUTION CONSULTANT (AND HOW TO AVOID THESE MISTAKES)

Here are some mistakes that, if you know about them ahead of time, you might be able to prevent making:

Mistake 1: Thinking strategy development and strategy execution are the same

The work required to develop your strategy and the work required to execute your strategy clearly will be different. It's important that those executing the initiatives that make up the strategy execution engagement appreciate the details of the strategy and recognize that these are two stages of work. First, your strategy is developed and you and your team will reach consensus about what you will set as strategic goals. Secondly, your whole team engages to execute the strategy—which make take a multiple year effort.

Mistake 2: Assuming any consultant that can create your strategy also has the skills to execute it

The main message for you here is to check with your consulting partner to understand their strengths and their limitations. It's possible that you can use the same consulting partner for your strategy development and execution, but it is also certainly possible that the consultants that help you create your strategy do not have the skill sets to help with the new obligations of a full-blown execution. Ask questions about this approach to helping you execute your strategy so that you're comfortable you have the right consulting partner.

Mistake 3: Investing in strategy development but not strategy execution

The big risk of investing in strategy development, but then not investing in the execution support, is that you end up with a wonderful strategy document tucked away in a binder on a bookshelf. It's the day-to-day activities where your teams are driving the most important priority initiatives that will provide the progress and the traction that will deliver the results you want as you execute your strategy. If your team is not highly skilled at driving large initiatives and delivering breakthrough results then go get a consultant to help you.

Mistake 4: Driving strategy execution without verifying you have a viable strategy

This mistake is actually the opposite of mistake #3. It's important to make sure that you are executing the right set of initiatives. It won't do you well to create awesome project results that don't turn into the financial performance you desire or don't position you in your marketplace for long-term success. Pause your frenetic activity to review your strategy to check that it still makes sense. You should do that annually. If you're not convinced then you might need to redo your strategy exercise. An outside consultant can provide an independent perspective to help you decide if your strategy is solid or needs some adjustment.

One of my mentors was Dr. W. Edwards Deming, the American expert on statistical methods to guide production and deliver high quality. He told the story of the Pontiac Fiero as a production line that had flawless quality processes and excellent production methods that were created by the execution of an approach to drive operations excellence. The Fiero disappeared after only five years of production, however, because of mismanagement and the lack of a comprehensive strategy. You can prevent this situation from happening on your watch by ensuring you have a viable strategy in the first place (and THEN follow a rigorous strategy execution process).

OTHER POSSIBLE CONSULTING SUPPORT THAT ALIGNS WITH STRATEGY

Remember your company might engage consultants for support in any area within your business. Sometimes the need arises when your business follows a strategy execution process and identifies some shortcomings or subpar results. When your team has a gap in capability or the ability to deliver results is not up to your expectations, this might be a signal to bring a consultant in to help with a specific project or set of initiatives.

Any of this consulting work that follows because of the strategy execution process could broadly be considered under the execution umbrella, but we categorized these engagements separately. For example, let's say you identify leadership deficiencies. This might trigger a leadership development engagement. You might be bumping into cultural barriers that are frustrating you and your team and hampering their ability to make progress. A culture-shifting engagement with a consulting partner might be in order. If you're having operational challenges, then the types of engagements that you might solicit consulting support could include Lean process improvement, overall equipment effectiveness, or other operations excellence principles.

Another example, if you have a poor underperforming website or see an opportunity to leverage social media, but you are not doing anything in that area now, then you might require consultant support for search engine optimization or social media performance. All of these examples are simply illustrating that there are lots of other types of engagements that can broadly fall under strategy execution.

SUMMARY POINTS

- Strategic goals should align with your company's vision and force you to stretch outside your comfort zone.
- With your consulting partner, *strategy engagement* elements could include a deep review of your: financials, market position, and market

trends, as well as a review of technology and recommendations about products and services, geographies, and recommendations for areas of development within the company.

- A *strategy execution engagement* consists of converting your strategy into strategic goals, cascading those goals throughout the organization, defining specific initiatives, creating a rhythm of progress review sessions, guiding problem solving, and mentoring leaders and "accountable metric owners."

- But tread lightly: the same consulting partner may not be capable of doing both strategy development and strategy execution. And you do need both. Having a viable strategy is the primary action, followed by execution.

Watch the bonus video for this chapter at the companion website for this book:

http://www.TheStopWastingMoneyBook.com

15

Leadership and Leadership Development Consulting Engagements

Leadership development represents all the collective activities you would employ to improve the effectiveness of your leadership team within your organization. This also includes those people without formal leadership titles but who lead teams of people or play roles of informal leaders among their peers.

Leadership is the idea of getting your team excited and inspired to play at the highest level. It is about making great decisions, including the challenging difficult ones where you are faced with choices that look like viable options, yet you only have the resources and capacity to choose one of them. Leadership is operating at high integrity and aligning with the company's values, purpose, vision, and mission and is about insuring your team embraces and embodies these principles as well.

Leadership development is about making all of this happen more effectively. It includes bringing new leaders along and preparing future leaders for their roles. Leadership development also recognizes the informal leaders in your company and gives them tools and builds their capabilities to provide more positive impact for your company. These people could be in temporary leadership roles of project teams, or they could be influential employees who lack a formal title. A great leadership development program will include all of your formal and informal leaders.

THE HISTORY OF LEADERSHIP DEVELOPMENT CONSULTING

Historically, leadership development consulting consisted only of leadership training programs. Many of those programs were off-site where individual managers were sent to learn certain skill sets. In fact, the earliest programs were more about management skills than leadership. The difference between management and leadership basically comes down to foundational elements of the job and how to ensure the job is done correctly and on time versus leadership elements where you are inspiring and enabling your team to play at the highest level.

Over time, different assessment tools were added into leadership consulting engagements. Some popular ones are DiSC, Hermann Brain Dominance Index, Myers-Briggs Type Indicator, and various 360-degree surveys. Each of these provides insight to help the individual leader appreciate their strengths and weaknesses and how they act in different situations. A 360-degree feedback survey also provides insight to how other people in the organization perceive them. Today, leadership development consulting includes training and mentoring with observations and feedback to go along with the assessment work.

UNIQUE LEADERSHIP DEVELOPMENT CONSULTANT ATTRIBUTES

Consultants who support you in your leadership development need to have a few additional skill sets beyond what other consultants may require. These include:

The ability to train others and communicate in a group setting

Training is common across many consulting engagements. What's important for your consultants to have as part of their skill repertoire as a leadership development trainer is to find the right balance of leadership principles and real examples for your leadership team to work on. You want to have a set of principles for the leaders to embrace. Because adults are experiential learners, they need to build in exercises for the leaders to apply the principles so that your training is not simply an academic exercise. Then they demonstrate the principles in action with examples of other leaders who have success stories to share. In fact, if you have some success stories of those principles in action by leaders from within your company then your consulting partner will have the highest credibility with your team. If you engage them for an extended period of time this should be easy.

Real experience as a leader

It's extremely difficult for those your consulting partner is developing to become effective leaders to see him/her as a credible resource if he/she doesn't have direct leadership experience. A leadership development consultant needs to respond to challenging questions and add to the discussion with their own personal experience having solved similar leadership challenges in the past. This is a higher skill than a trainer who is able to present material without adding elements of this personal experience.

The ability to coach and mentor

Coaching in general is an important consulting skill that applies in many consulting engagements. Within leadership development, mentoring is a critical skill as the consultant must be able to monitor behaviors, model the same behaviors with their own examples, and role play on the spot, as well as provide feedback and suggest course corrections to the person in the leadership role. Coaching skills are also critically important. Coaches typically guide self-discovery through their questions and probing and suggestions for ideas to apply. The astute coach must guide this introspective self-discovery process to make sure the lessons the leader learns are the right ones to further their development and effectiveness and a leader.

Leadership development engagements may also include facilitating the various assessments and making observations of particular leaders as they hold meetings or other interactions with their teams. It's more than just facilitating these assessments, however. The assessments will indicate areas of strength and opportunities for development. Those areas that are identified as development needs become the agenda of your consulting partner to work with as they mentor and coach in these one-on-one situations.

Another element of leadership development consulting is the deliberate tie to the company's purpose, vision, mission, and values, as well as specifically defined attributes of your company's desired culture. It helps when it's the same consulting partner who has the skill sets to operate and support you in both your culture shifting and leadership development work. It's the role of individual leaders to make sure that your company team members embrace and learn to live the values and desired cultural attributes on a daily basis. Further, it's their job to reemphasize your company's purpose, vision, and mission at every opportunity to communicate with your team. Your consulting partner can help mentor leaders to help them emphasize and support your culture.

WHY YOU SHOULD CONSIDER LEADERSHIP DEVELOPMENT SUPPORT

In the spirit of continuously investing in your people for their ongoing improvement and learning, leadership development will be a constant element of your business transformation agenda to make sure that you are always positioning your team members to become the best that they can be. With that said, there are some specific indicators that leadership development consulting may be right for you, for the following reasons:

Your leadership team is unclear about expectations

You may find yourself in a position where it's time to communicate a full set of new expectations on your leadership team, more aligned with new leadership principles that are not present in your business today. It may be that you had recent leadership turnover, that you had to upgrade your talent deliberately, or that your existing leadership team that has been in place for quite some time needs the periodic focus and reminder to upgrade their skills.

Unacceptable turnover

When employees choose to leave your company to go somewhere else, it can be an indicator that there's an issue within your organization to solve. Some people do leave jobs to seek higher opportunities that they believe are absent from their current position. As Jim Harter and Amy Adkins report in their February 24, 2017 Business Journal on Gallup.com, only 33% of employees are engaged in their jobs, which gives them reason to consider switching. And when employees do switch, 91% of them leave their company. Talk about disruptive! When you conduct your exit interviews with people who have chosen to leave, you may find that there are leadership challenges within your company, which will indicate leadership development consulting can help you.

You observe unacceptable leadership behavior

Naturally you and any good leader would want to intervene immediately when they see behavior that is not acceptable or aligned with your highest expectations. What's required, however, may be more than just you having a quick conversation with an individual. What you have observed may be the tip of the iceberg compared to a more systemic style that people within your company use when leading others. This can be especially true in times of stressful situations and challenges. That unacceptable behavior may be a lack of alignment between individuals, actions, and your company's purpose, vision, mission and values. The leadership development program is an opportunity to correct this.

You're not pleased with the results

When results are lagging versus your expectations, there could be many root causes and problems to solve. If there are result shortfalls in a particular team or department or even more broadly across your whole business, this could be an opportunity for you to inject some new leadership principles into how your leaders inspire and motivate their team to the next higher level of performance. There may be other challenges, problems to solve, or processes to improve, so don't ignore them and think that leadership development alone will solve this—but leadership development could be a huge element. The best situation would be for your consulting partner to be able to assist with a wide range of problem solving and process improvement, and inject leadership development within the broader engagement.

POTENTIAL ELEMENTS OF A LEADERSHIP DEVELOPMENT ENGAGEMENT

Many of these potential elements have been described in this chapter already, but I will still itemize them here for you.

Assessments

Your consulting partner might use a leadership development assessment tool to help raise the awareness of individuals and your collective team to provide some data based insights about styles, strengths, and weaknesses. DISC, Herman Brain Dominance Index, and Myers-Briggs Type Indicator are some of the popular ones. They may also a 360-degree feedback process to collect data.

Observations

The consultant may join in critical meetings to act as an observer. What they are likely looking for include leadership presence, how leaders communicate, and how their teams respond to them. They may also make observations by training a leader as they go through their day-to-day routines.

Training

Depending on the needs identified there may be some training programs that are best communicated and deployed across your leadership team through formal training sessions. The best method of training is a mixture of formal training sessions and implementation time so that the leaders can apply the principles that they've learned in real situations.

Mentoring and Coaching

While your consultant may work with groups of people in a formal setting, it's also possible that they will spend some one-on-one time with different individuals to help deepen the experience in applying the leadership principles. This works extremely well when paired with formal training methods. You might see a leadership development agenda that spans months as your consultant conducts training exercises then mentors their leadership students in the real world day-to-day situations they are faced with. This pattern will iterate and continue throughout a whole suite of leadership agenda topics and across multiple leadership groups.

Organization Feedback

Your consultant may also provide structured feedback about the skill levels of your leadership team members and also about their observations regarding high-potential team members who may be ready to step into their first or next leadership role. The probability exists that you may have a high contributing employee who is in a leadership position who frankly does not have the leadership skills, but was promoted into that role of managing a team because it seemed to be the right next move. Your consulting partner may have a perspective about that "misfit" person who might have a better role without the requirement of leading people.

Set Up an Internal Leadership University

Many companies standardize their set of leadership principles and the training that they believe is important to have as part of their university. For example, training in communication skills or how to best motivate and inspire your team might be mandatory for every person in a leadership role. How to build trust in your organization through your actions and your behaviors, how to develop trust across your team, and how a leader mentors their team members might be other topics for trainings. Mentoring and coaching skills may be a class within a leadership university. Naturally, these can be tailored depending on the given leadership challenges and aspirations that you have within your company.

SUMMARY POINTS

- Leadership development brings new leaders along, prepares future leaders for their roles, and recognizes informal leaders in your company—giving them the tools to build their capabilities which in turn positively impacts your company.
- Third party consultants assist when your leadership team is unclear about expectations, or when the company is experiencing unacceptable turnover, poor leadership behavior, or less than satisfactory results.
- A Leadership Development Engagement is comprised of many elements, such as: assessments, observations, training, mentoring and coaching, and organization feedback and the creation of an internal leadership university.

Watch the bonus video for this chapter at the companion website for this book:

http://www.TheStopWastingMoneyBook.com

16

Culture-Shifting Consulting Engagements

Your company culture is represented by the sum total of all of the individual people who work at your company. It consists of their behaviors and actions which are a function of their beliefs and thought processes. The reason that understanding your culture is so important is that this invisible energy in your company has the power to accelerate your progress towards your strategic goals. Or it could do just the opposite and knock your progress off track all together.

Over time, your culture will evolve depending on the people who work in your company. As new people are hired, they bring with them their particular sets of beliefs and thought processes and the associated actions and behaviors. Naturally, people in leadership positions have more ability to shape your culture because your leaders will reward behaviors. The rewarded behavior will catch the attention of others, and they will slowly begin to mold and modify their behavior accordingly.

Culture shifting is the idea that you can design and move your culture from what it is today to something that better aligns with what you want to experience in your company in the future.

Cultures will naturally evolve, but that takes an extreme amount of time. And without the proper guidance, the culture may evolve in a direction that is unproductive or unfavorable for what it is you really desire. It's best to take a proactive stance. For the sake of this discussion about consulting support, let's define culture shifting as those initiatives designed to create the culture that you want to have and shift from your current state culture to the desirable culture.

HISTORY OF CULTURE-SHIFTING CONSULTING

Compared to strategy consulting, which has been around for nearly 100 years, culture-shifting consulting is relatively new. While the idea of culture as a driving and individual force in your organization is gaining some traction and awareness, the need to proactively do something about culture has only recently hit the main stream.

The early days of culture-shifting consulting were really more human resources consulting or leadership development training programs. Even in Lean process improvement and operations excellence consulting, culture is named a positive byproduct as you improve other areas of the company. So as you improve leadership skill or learn to engage employees in making operational improvements, you can expect to see a positive change in your culture along the way. While historically the "culture" was something that people blamed in their organizations for lack of performance, today, progressive leaders are looking to gain help in shifting their cultures proactively to shape the results they desire. Some consulting companies have culture shifting as part of their service offering as they think more holistically about improving company performance or about business transformation. Other consulting firms focus narrowly on culture, which sometimes includes teamwork and leadership.

UNIQUE ELEMENTS OF CULTURE-SHIFTING ENGAGEMENTS

To be effective at shifting a company's culture, you need to understand the behaviors and motivations of the full population for that company or group. This is not about process improvement in one small area that impacts only a handful of people—as part of your business transformation you need your whole culture to support you.

Remember, the company's culture is the sum of all employees' beliefs, thoughts, and behaviors. It's important to have your consulting partner help you understand exactly what those beliefs, thoughts, and behaviors are so that you can determine whether or not there are interventions required to move your company culture towards what it is you wish to have in place. Just as in many other types of consulting engagements, you can expect analysis, surveys, interviews, and observations. In this case, the analysis, surveys, interviews, and observations are completed with your company culture in mind—which implies looking at the collective behavior of individuals. Naturally, there will be some work with the leadership team to give direct feedback about what the consultants are finding, and to also help facilitate decisions about what culture attributes are desirable. This is one type of consulting engagement where you are likely to require that all employees are surveyed as part of the data collection and analysis.

WHY YOU SHOULD CONSIDER CULTURE-SHIFTING SUPPORT

If you're not getting the results you want, then your culture may be at least part of the problem. Further, if you are achieving the desired results, but at great cost as your team struggles to brute force their way through, then culture may also be part of that particular issue.

Begin with some introspection. Take a look at yourself and your team and ask, "Do you have an unacceptable level of frustration regarding getting things done in your company?" Is it the rate of progress or is it the inability of teams to work effectively? Are there undesirable behaviors like backstabbing or talking down about other people? Do you observe a lack of initiative or a lack of trust? These may all be attributes of your current existing culture. Another indicator that your culture is having issues is if you're experiencing burnout on your team or higher than expected turnover.

If one or more of these conditions exist, then it's time to enlist some external support.

Culture shifting is usually bigger than what an individual executive business leader or team can pull off by themselves. The unfortunate reality about culture is that the people leading the company may actually have some blind spots about how they act in different situations that adds to the negative cultural dynamics. This is why it's so critical for a skilled independent consulting team to help you solve this problem.

POTENTIAL ELEMENTS OF A CULTURE-SHIFTING ENGAGEMENT

As with many consulting engagements of every type, the likely first step is an assessment of where you are today. This could include reviewing your existing data, creating a survey, interviewing key employees, making observations within meetings, and other work place dynamics. Then it's time to pull together the findings into a collective report of what your current state culture attributes look like.

Management workshops

It's important for the leadership team of your company to proactively decide what you want your culture to look like. You can do this with the information about your current culture based on the assessment or you accomplish this by looking forward into what you want to create in the future regarding your organizations culture. The consultants will lead exercises to help gain consensus momentum for the management team. While there is no limit to the number of specific attributes you can choose to define your culture, you will want to have a list that can be remembered and articulated by your employees.

Align your culture with your company's purpose, vision, mission, and core values

If you do not have alignment or consensus about your purpose, vision, mission, and values then you absolutely must start here. Your consulting partner will help facilitate discussions and the decision-making process so that you have a complete reset and consensus about those critical elements of who you are and why you are here as a company.

Compare existing to desirable attributes

There are a number of ways that your consulting partner can help you identify which of those desirable attributes need the most work, often using a combination of surveys, interviews, and observations. Once you have a sense of this prioritization you know which areas deserve focus for the immediate timeframe.

Launching Initiatives

The desired attributes with the largest gap from current state to desired state are the areas where clearly defined initiatives are required to assist in installing the behaviors that align with the attribute. For example, if high trust is the desired attribute, yet your company is experiencing a current culture of low trust, then you have to create a number of trust-building initiatives across your organization.

Connecting Your Culture

It's important that your culture is not isolating, but is connected to a number of the other parts of your business. This includes your desired results and the performance you expect to see, your strategy and your strategic priorities, and your leadership development programs and other team building activities that you have planned for your company. Indeed, you want to reinforce your desired culture in all of your business activities.

COSTLY MISTAKES WHEN CHOOSING A CULTURE-SHIFTING CONSULTANT—AND HOW TO AVOID THEM

Culture is an interesting element of your company because it is invisible. It is not like observing a production line to identify where the waste is. It's not analyzing numbers on a spreadsheet or looking at your financial statements. It's appreciating the inner dynamics of your organization. Basically, how stuff gets done—which is a complex function of your multiple teams of people and the jobs that they are assigned.

There are many consultants who have strong analytical horsepower and know how to make direct observations, notice when processes are not working correctly, or are wizards with financial statements. In addition to the above, in order to be effective at shifting culture, your consulting partner needs to appreciate people dynamics, mainly leadership, teamwork, and culture attributes. It's imperative that they understand the dynamics of human interaction and motivation. They need to appreciate how beliefs are formed, how beliefs guide thoughts processes, and how thoughts turn into behaviors and actions—many of which by the way are unconscious human behaviors.

With these factors in mind, it's possible to make some costly mistakes when you choose your culture-shifting consultant. Take a look at the following list of mistakes and the suggestions of how you can avoid them.

Not Differentiating Theory Versus Experience

Every consultant in every area of improving your business will bump into your culture. They may even make remarks about the need for you to shift or change your culture in order for you to be successful for the long term. Your task before asking that same consultant to assist you in shifting your culture is to confirm what their approach is and whether or not they have actually done this before. There are plenty of books and blog posts that someone can read about changing culture. The trick is trusting that your consulting partner can actually help you guide your culture shift.

No Courage with Giving Leadership Feedback

Culture shifting is an important part of your leadership teams' role. Your leadership team needs to be able to receive feedback from your consulting partner. Equally important, though, is that your consulting partner must have the courage to say what needs to be said to you and your leadership team. Some of your leaders may be part of the culture problem, or at least might be contributing in unproductive ways. To accelerate culture change requires leadership alignment and awareness. You want your consultant to help build that leadership awareness which sometimes means having difficult conversations, perhaps with the person who hired them.

Overuse of External Benchmarks

Culture benchmarks can be useful, but internal progress is the first priority. The best results come from looking at benchmarks specifically designed around your desired culture attributes and analyzing how you are doing versus where the company stands in regards to those desired attributes today. You want to measure this internal benchmark to receive the feedback of a proper sense of progress—and where there is still work to be done. Once you've made significant progress with your internal benchmarks, you might consider comparing your company to the outside world, but only after your internal progress has been significant.

SUMMARY POINTS

- Culture shifting requires that you design and move your culture from what it is today to something that better aligns with what you want to experience in your company in the future.
- Your consulting partner can help you understand exactly what your company beliefs, thoughts, and behaviors are so that you can move your company culture towards what it is you wish to have in place.
- There's a saying that a fish can't see the water they swim in. So it is for the business leader and his/her culture. A skilled independent consulting team brings awareness to negative cultural dynamics.
- Consultants are trained to ferret out the unconscious human behaviors that drive the dynamics between team members and the executive team.

Watch the bonus video for this chapter at the companion website for this book:

http://www.TheStopWastingMoneyBook.com

17

Consulting Engagements to Implement Lean Thinking and Improve Day-to-Day Execution

In the 1950s, post-war Japan was a wreck, and the mighty Unites States was an economic powerhouse. Japanese quality of exports was poor and not respected by US consumers. Out of competitive necessity, Toyota Motor Corporation under the guidance of Taiichi Ohno began what is now known as the Toyota Production System (TPS).

Ohno guided Toyota as an executive on their journey of continuous process improvement. He incessantly searched for more efficient ways to produce with higher quality, and with shorter lead times. From this he developed a set of principles that define TPS.

Interestingly, the origins of some of the ideas that Ohno tried and implemented were actually originally developed in the United States. Look at these examples:

- Henry Ford developed the first assembly line, a concept that Toyota expanded.
- My mentor, Dr. W. Edwards Deming, was another huge influence on Toyota, especially with the Plan-Do-Check-Act Cycle (PDCA).
- The US government's training program, Training within Industry, also led Toyota to understand the importance of standardized work.
- As Ohno was trying to figure out a solution to inventory management challenges, he observed the restocking of shelves in American supermarkets which led to developing "kanban" and pull systems.

(Note: Deming called PDCA the Shewhart Cycle after the father of statistical quality control, Walter Shewhart. Others call PDCA the Deming Cycle, as Deming popularized the approach. Deming actually preferred PDSA, where S is for Study rather than Check, as he believed this step is about analysis and reflection rather than inspection. Many people also call A "Adjust", as you are making adjustments based on what you learned in the Check or Study phase. No matter what you choose to call it, recognize that PDCA is an important concept!)

WHAT LEAN IS

Lean is the name given to the operating philosophy based on the Toyota Production System. It is a way of thinking, along with supporting tools and methods that enables you to provide the highest quality product or service in the shortest possible time, in the most efficient way possible. Doesn't every business strive for this!

Lean Thinking, which originated with TPS, is guided by a number of basic principles that, through decades of experimentation and application in a variety of situations and industries, have proven to solidly deliver on the quality, delivery, and cost promise above.

From these principles emerged a number of Lean tools that practitioners have learned to use as a way to train implementation teams and apply the principles. For example, the tool kanban supports the principle that it is best to pull work from a previous process, rather than that process push their work to the next before it's ready. I'll share more on Lean Thinking versus tools in the next section. For now, recognize there is a logical linkage.

Here is a list of a few of the principles about TPS and Lean as described in Jeffrey Liker's book, *The Toyota Way:*

- Base management decisions on long-term philosophy, even at the expense of short-term goals

- Building the foundation for continuous improvement and employee empowerment with standardized tasks
- Use only reliable, thoroughly tested, technology
- Grow leaders who thoroughly understand the work, live the philosophy, and teach it to others
- Develop exceptional people and teams who follow your company's philosophy
- Respect your network of partners and suppliers by challenging and helping them improve
- Make decisions slowly by consensus, considering all options; implement decisions rapidly
- Become a learning organization through relentless reflection and continuous improvement

WASTE ELIMINATION

One of Ohno's drivers was the relentless elimination of anything that did not add value from the perspective of the customer. This led to his definitions of seven types of waste that was instrumental in developing the way organizations identify non-value-add work. Ohno's "Seven Wastes" model has become core practice in many academic approaches. These wastes can be remembered with the acronym, TIM WOOD.

- *Transportation*—moving parts does not add value to the parts, just the cost to move them
- *Inventory*—any inventory beyond the minimum you need for you current job, right now.
- *Motion*—unnecessary or excessive movement.
- *Waiting*—delay, waiting, or time spent in a queue with no value being added.
- *Overproduction*—producing more that you need right now.
- *Over processing*—undertaking extra work at extra cost that does not add value or value proportionate to the extra cost.

- *Defects*—any quality problem, which then leads to scrap or rework (other non-value work).

In recent years, an eighth waste, *Skill*, has been added to the list, which is the waste of people's talent by not involving them, tapping into their ideas, nor getting them engaged. (This makes the acronym TIM WOODS.)

A BREAKTHROUGH BOOK: *LEAN THINKING*

In 1990, James Womack and Daniel Jones released a book called, *The Machine that Changed the World*. This book was a case study about Toyota and how they literally created a breakthrough with their production system, TPS.

They then followed up with their book, *Lean Thinking: Banish Waste and Create Wealth in Your Corporation*, in 1996. In *Lean Thinking*, Womack and Jones coined the phrase "Lean" that we are widely familiar with today. The book dives deep into a number of example companies that were recognized for their successful implementation of Lean principles to transform their operations and their full companies. This is an important book because very few companies are able to go all the way with Lean implementation. Most get sidetracked along the way and fail to fully realize the full benefit that Lean Thinking offers.

(Note: One of the companies highlighted, *The Wiremold Company*, is perhaps the best-known example of a full company Lean transformation. The enterprise-wide change was exciting, and I had the pleasure of being part of executing the implementation strategy for ten years early in my career.)

Today, even though there are more examples of successful Lean stories, the philosophy is still quite different from traditional business and therefore very challenging to learn and apply. At the root of any Lean effort, the company's aim is to improve quality, cost, and delivery to the customer by a relentless focus on:

- Decreasing *waste*
- Reducing *variability*

- Increasing *flexibility*
- Developing a *Lean Thinking Mindset* as you engage all of your employees on your journey.

LEAN APPLIES IN EVERY INDUSTRY

While the core elements of Lean were born in automotive manufacturing, they quickly spread to other discrete part manufacturing and then process industries in the 1990s. By the 2000s, Lean had emerged into banking, insurance, health care, retail, and many other service industries. Additionally, back-office processes like accounting can become way more efficient using Lean principles.

Today, you can find examples of Lean Thinking virtually anywhere. When you stick to the core as described above, any company can benefit from the huge potential that implementing Lean creates for you.

WHY LEAN THINKING IS MORE IMPORTANT THAN LEAN TOOLS

> *"Just as a carpenter needs a vision of what to build in order to get the full benefit of a hammer, Lean Thinkers need a vision before picking up our Lean tools," said Womack (author of* Lean Thinking*). "Thinking deeply about purpose, process, people is the key to doing this."*
>
> ~ FROM THE LEAN ENTERPRISE INSTITUTE, INC. WEBSITE

Many companies hear about some of the Lean tools such as 5S, SMED (Single-Minute Exchange of Dies), kanban, Value Stream Mapping, takt time, level production, standardized work, poke yoke, heijunka, TPM, Hoshin Kanri, visual management, PDCA, and other tools. All of these are important components of a Lean operating system, whether used in manufacturing, health care, financial services, retail, or in any other environment.

The problem is that implementing the tools without understanding the principles behind the tools is limiting, suboptimal, and risky. I know of examples where a company asks a consultant to come facilitate a team-based improvement activity (kaizen event) to implement one of the tools. The consultant happily complies, only to realize later that the benefit would be limited because their company lacked other critical parts of what really needs to be an integrated production system. The risk is that the company thinks they are implementing Lean, but then wonders where the impact is.

Here's a case example to illustrate this point: I was brought in to review a company that reported they had been implementing Lean for about two years. They had a major campaign to implement 5S in all areas of the plant, but that was the only Lean tool they had implemented. When you walked through the plant, you were impressed with how clean and orderly it was. Unfortunately, the signs of traditional manufacturing were everywhere, with lots of inventory, production lines that were clearly over-staffed, lines frequently stopping, production workers walking around trying to find a way to keep busy, etc. To top it off, the senior manager in charge of the site commented they have not received the ROI from Lean yet. Ouch!

APPRECIATE THE PRINCIPLES BEHIND THE TOOLS FIRST

Rather than base your implementation on tools only, and certainly don't take each Lean tool and roll it out everywhere one at a time, the better approach is to first appreciate the Lean principles behind the tools to guide your thinking of how to apply Lean. How did the tool become what it is, and why is it important?

For example, many people have the incorrect perspective that the tool kanban is what this Lean implementation is all about. They make implementing kanban stores of inventory between production steps a priority, and diligently design the kanban cards to match their limited understanding of kanban.

What they don't realize is that the ultimate situation is to flow the production without needing kanban in the first place. Where you can't flow production from one step to the next, then kanban may be a reasonable answer, but how much inventory do you need? Do you do a two-bin system or have multiple bins? How many kanban cards should be in circulation? Where should the kanban store be located; at the supplier process or the customer process? The right answers are based on a number of complex variables, which is why it's critical to know the principles behind the tools and get help from the right expert who has a Lean Thinking perspective beyond just the tools.

As you evaluate your potential consulting partner, make sure that they deeply understand the lean principles and how to apply those principles in your company. Engaging them in dialogue about your biggest challenges and see if you are inspired by their thinking about what to do and why.

CREATE AN INTEGRATED PRODUCTION SYSTEM

As quoted in *The Toyota Way* by Jeffrey Liker, Fujio Cho, President of Toyota Motor Corporation says, *"The key to Toyota Way and what makes Toyota stand out is not any of the individual elements. But what is important is having all the elements together as a system. It must be practiced every day in a very consistent manner—not in spurts."*

What makes the Lean principles so exciting is how they can enable your complete business transformation. As you implement these principles holistically in your business, you will experience a huge breakthrough in performance.

The other thing to realize is that the tools are really implementation methods toward the aim of creating an integrated production system that has an inter-relationship and dependency across the different principles. There's no real value to taking one tool and applying it everywhere.

The right way to apply the different Lean tools is to first have a clear understanding of what the potential integrated production system would look like, and that usually requires outside expertise in the form of an expert Lean consultant who is skilled in production system design. This future state of your potential production system will then dictate a set of initiatives and an implementation sequence where you would then apply the different tools in the right order to assemble the building blocks of your future state. It's a process that has multiple iterations and will require support as you encounter interesting, challenging, and unexpected problems along the journey.

For example, when the pressure to generate quick revenue is high, do you abandon your production system design and throw temporary labor into the fray to produce and ship as much as you can? How do you know the right answer? (Hint: understanding takt time, a critical Lean principle, will help and can determine the required staffing level.) Don't abandon the principles. Let Lean Thinking guide you through these challenges.

To illustrate some of the challenges and complexities that exist when applying Lean Thinking to create your future production system, consider tools like takt time and level production. Takt time is the tool that represents the rate of sales and is a critical input to your production cell or line design. Level production is to smooth out spikes in demand and make the production schedule smooth rather than choppy, which is a huge enabler for other elements of your production system.

In a static environment, these tools are simple and powerful. But, what do you do if you're in an environment with highly seasonal demand, where a significant amount of your annual sales occurs between Black Friday and Christmas? Applying takt time and level production now takes on a new meaning. If you understand the principles behind the tools, you can design your production system to handle this interesting constraint in your environment. If you only know the tool but not the principles behind it, you'll be stuck and risk a poor design that is suboptimal.

You often have to get creative in how you apply the principles—it's how you have incorporated Lean into your thinking that really differentiates deep expert consultants. Lean is not a cookie-cutter implementation, which is why tools-only based consultants who have applied Lean in the just one environment within which they learned the Lean tools often struggle when they find themselves in a new industry or situation with twists or non-standard surprises like the above example.

Beware of consultants who talk only of the tools—they may not be as much help as you think.

HOW KAIZEN RELATES TO LEAN

Kaizen is a Japanese word that roughly translates to mean continuous improvement. The real essence of kaizen is to have a collective philosophy of constantly making small improvements that will accumulate over time to have significant impacts.

The need for kaizen is driven by a collective dissatisfaction with your current processes, and the art of constantly challenging the process to make things better.

Many people have heard the word kaizen and think that this is the same as Lean. While kaizen is used in many Lean implementations, it is an approach and philosophy that must be guided by the Lean principles.

There are different forms of formal kaizen, such as an organized team-based improvement activity, called *Kaizen Events*. Another form of kaizen is the suggestion system concept called *Kaizen Teian*, where people make suggestions and are encouraged to implement them. Informally, kaizen can happen by every employee every day as they make small changes in how they do things.

THE DIFFERENCE BETWEEN KAIZEN AND LEAN

Many people equate kaizen with Lean. Kaizen is a powerful implementation approach for sure, and many Lean implementations utilize kaizen events. The thing is, just because you're doing kaizen doesn't guarantee that you're implementing Lean. In fact, many companies have used kaizen effectively to engage employees and to gather their collective brainpower to solve problems but without infusing any Lean principles into the thought process. Their solution might work, but it is generally to optimize an existing process within the existing paradigms. With Lean principles injected into the thought process, the kaizen team will likely achieve results that simply blow away the current results.

Supporting kaizen teams is one of the common roles for a consultant who guides your Lean implementation. Teams need to learn the Lean principles and receive guidance in applying them in different challenging situations. Additionally, facilitated kaizen team events are a very effective way to march toward change that has significant results in a short period of time, especially when guided by a consultant who understands the principles you're implementing.

USE KAIZEN TO ACHIEVE YOUR STRATEGIC GOALS

Just as we described earlier that Lean Thinking with a production system perspective is critical, this remains paramount when planning kaizen events. While many companies launch countless kaizen teams to tackle improvements across their business, they later experience a disconnection between the aggregate results that the kaizen teams reported from the various events and the financial statements. The kaizen savings have not been integrated in a way that drives real operational improvement that the customer sees or that the company financials can verify.

For this reason, it is critical that you have clarity of your strategic goals and the initiatives that will enable you to build your future state production system and achieve those goals. If your consulting partner guides your strategy and strategy execution process, you can then identify where Kaizen is the best implementation method to add to your list of strategic initiatives. With these initiatives planned out, it will become clear that kaizen events can play a major role in implementing the changes you need to make your future state a reality.

Let kaizen be the way to engage employees toward delivering your future state production system, and first have the plan clearly defined so your kaizen events can have maximum impact.

KAIZEN EVENTS AND PDCA

As described in the earlier section, PDCA is a powerful concept. PDCA, or the Plan–Do–Check–Act cycle, is a continuous improvement framework where you essentially conduct a number of improvement experiments, adjusting the approach each subsequent time through the cycle. It closely follows the scientific method, which starts with a hypothesis and a plan. You then execute the plan (Do), and evaluate the results (Check). Then, based on what you learned during this cycle, you make adjustments and define your next action (Act), which leads to the next cycle.

Kaizen is the perfect process within which to conduct PDCA, as you might go through a number of PDCA cycles during a kaizen event. For example, in a changeover time reduction kaizen event, you are applying the principles of SMED to reduce your downtime due to changeover of a piece of equipment. You might do a number of trials during a week-long event while making changes to the tooling, designing standard work for the set-up operators, simplifying clamping, etc.

THE CORRECT WAY TO PRONOUNCE KAIZEN

One interesting point about how people pronounce the word kaizen is that the pronunciation actually matters. The second syllable, "zen," rhymes with the word "pen." Kai Zen means "continuous improvement," like we described above.

Many people pronounce the second syllable as "zan" or "zahn." I had to check with a friend who worked for Toyota in Japan to see if this meant something different, and he confirmed that not only is the meaning different, but it is a negative meaning. Kai Zan means to "manipulate or falsify." Oops—that's not what we want!

For this reason, we suggest you pay attention to how the people on your team pronounce the word kaizen, and correct people so that they are engaging in the desired practice and using the correct word to describe it! And listen carefully to make sure your consultant is pronouncing this correctly, too! Words have power!

FULL LEAN IMPLEMENTATION BRINGS HUGE ROI

While many companies choose to implement a few of the Lean tools and see some benefit, there is a pot of gold available to those who go for a full, enterprises-wide Lean implementation. Two favorite examples are Danaher and The Wiremold Company. I'm personally familiar with both companies and their philosophies and approaches, given I worked with both during my career.

DANAHER

In the 1980s, Danaher began to embrace Lean in its Jacobs Vehicle Systems division, located in Bloomfield, Connecticut. As the results began to excite the executive team, Danaher expanded implementation across all its businesses.

The "Danaher Business System" (DBS) was born, and Lean tools and approaches began to modify principles and methods to drive results, and then to standardize their application across Danaher companies.

Over twenty-five years later, DBS continues to provide a strategic advantage to Danaher—one that Wall Street has rewarded handsomely. Danaher's 2016 Annual Report illustrates how its 5-year cumulative Total Shareholder Return has significantly outpaced the S&P 500 and their peer industry indexes.

Danaher continues to credit DBS as a main driver of their financial performance. You can find language in nearly every annual report and press release that acknowledges DBS. For example, its December 15, 2016 press release to provide Wall Street with their 2017 financial outlook says, "With the Danaher Business System as our driving force and competitive advantage…"

In another example, Danaher's 2012 annual report describes how central DBS has become to drive improvements and results across all areas of their business:

> At Danaher, Lean truly is a core operating philosophy that guides every process and every employee. While Danaher's aggressive growth has challenged their company, with DBS, they continue to perform well and achieve great results that have led to outstanding financials.

Clearly, Danaher is one example of a company that demonstrates how practicing Lean well can make a huge difference for your business.

THE WIREMOLD COMPANY

In 1991, Wiremold hired Art Byrne, its first CEO hired from the outside. Art is credited with bringing Lean principles to Jake Brake and Danaher and when hired looked to repeat the success story at Wiremold.

Despite barely making profit, when Art arrived he moved aggressively with a huge investment in consulting support to drive results as quickly as possible. In fact, a significant portion of the company's profits in the first one to two years was invested in consulting support for Lean implementation, which Wiremold called the Wiremold Production System.

Within a few years, the results had caught the attention of authors James Womack and Daniel Jones, and they were featured in the breakthrough book I mentioned earlier, *Lean Thinking*. Other books soon followed, such as *Gemba Kaizen*, by Masaki Imai. Before the end of the decade, the company had won the prestigious Shingo Prize for manufacturing excellence and was enjoying high levels of employee satisfaction, customer service, and financial performance.

The important thing to recognize is Wiremold's story was not just how they transformed manufacturing, but its entire business. All the operations functions were integrated into line-of-product teams. The production system enabled frequent shipments to customers, and the sales approach was modified to adjust customers' ordering behavior. New Product Development teams included design engineering, marketing, and operations. Financial processes were simplified as complexity in all areas of the business was systematically reduced.

After Art Byrne retired from Wiremold, he wrote a book that highlighted Wiremold's journey called *The Lean Turnaround*. He writes, "Wiremold achieved outstanding financial results by focusing on process improvement, and not forcing monthly financial targets."

Here are some statistics about Wiremold's results fro 1991-2000 he shares that will absolutely blow you away:

- *Lead-time* dropped from 4 to 6 weeks to 1 to 2 days
- *Customer Service* went from 50% to 98%
- *Productivity* went up 162%
- *Sales* quadrupled
- *EBITDA margin* went from 6.2% to 20.8%
- *Gross Profit* went from 38% to 51%
- *Working Capital / Sale* decreased from 21.8% to 6.7%
- *Operating Income* went up 13.4 times
- *Inventory Turns* went from 3 times to 18 times
- *Sales per Full-time Employee* (000's) went from 92 to 241
- *New Product Development Cycle Time* (median) went from 2-3 years to 3-12 months
- *Enterprise value* went up 2,467%

If these results don't convince you to invest heavily in implementing Lean as a core strategy in your business transformation over the next ten years, I don't know what will!

A Quick Personal Story

When I interviewed at McKinsey and Company to join the elite Lean Manufacturing/Operations Strategy and Excellence practice, I met with Peter Willats, who was the co-founder of the Kaizen Institute of Europe. He started our conversation with, "Now that we know that a kaizen event consulting approach simply doesn't work…"

To me, those were fighting words because I had just spent a decade at Wiremold where it appeared kaizen events were the core implementation approach that created the best full-enterprise Lean success story in history, anywhere on the globe! He went on to describe what happens to most companies and that Wiremold was a special exception that was doing a lot more than kaizen events that might be invisible to those who did not know what to look for.

By the end of our conversation, I understood his point and was a firm believer that he was right. He had demonstrated that because kaizen events as the consulting model—in the absence of other critical elements we've discussed in this chapter—would put too much burden on the client and not provide enough guidance to your leadership and resources, making the probability of success was quite low.

Now that I've gotten that out of the way, you should expect to have kaizen events be a central part of your consulting engagement when you implement Lean. Unless you are one of the lucky few who happen to have a CEO who has also successfully led a full-company transformation using Lean principles and is a fanatical supporter and driver, like Art Byrne of Wiremold, you will also need some consulting support to figure out your implementation strategy and then to drive all the implementation elements.

Of course, Art also invested $millions in consulting support on top of his direct leadership so success at the rate you desire will probably require consultants. The trick is to find the right ones. The rest of this chapter will help you know what to look for.

POTENTIAL ELEMENTS OF A LEAN CONSULTING ENGAGEMENT

While all the elements of a traditional consulting engagement may still be part of what you experience, here are some of the potential unique features of your Lean consulting engagement.

Conducting a Lean Assessment

This is a quick assessment to see how you stack up against a set of categories typical to a well-operating Lean environment. While this is interesting, remember the goal is to shift your business results, not to become Lean for Lean's sake. The Lean assessment exercise could lead you down that slippery slope if your consultant isn't clear that the purpose is to achieve great results.

Conducting an Operations Improvement Diagnostic

The operations improvement diagnostic is a critically important exercise to have conducted correctly so you can understand the current issues, design the potential future state, describe the activities and projects that will transform your operation, and to itemize the value at stake. It is typically 1-2 weeks in duration, but could also be 1-3 months to go deep with analysis and provide a detailed plan.

Training in the Variety of Lean Tools

Your teams will need to become proficient in understanding the principles behind the Lean tools and to apply them correctly. The consulting resource who will act as your sensei is responsible to guide your development. This is very much a "learn by doing" with mentoring and feedback approach toward mastery that will take time and repetition.

Leading the Annual and Monthly Strategic Goal Deployment™ (SGD™) Exercises

The SGD™ process goes by names such as Hoshin Kanri and policy deployment. This process helps you execute your strategy by aligning initiatives with your strategic goals, assign metrics and targets to the initiatives, develop action plans how you will achieve each set of targets, and create an infrastructure to monitor progress through the year. Note: This could be part of your strategy execution process.

Facilitating Kaizen Events

Ideally, your kaizen events align with the initiatives and targets identified in the Strategic Goal Deployment™. Your SGD™ action plans will contain kaizen events and other improvement projects. You will need help executing them and the consulting resource will train and facilitate your teams.

Owning Specific Initiatives, or Supporting the Client Team Leaders Across a Variety of Initiatives

Your consulting resource might take direct ownership for initiatives and conduct analyses or guide your team to execute the activities that will deliver the results.

Conducting Deep Analyses

There are many advanced methods that require deeper analyses, such as figuring out inventory stocking strategies using a "Plan For Every Part" (PFEP) methodology that then determines kanban quantities, etc. There are some advanced elements of your Lean strategy that you will want your consultant as an experienced Lean practitioner to do first, and then train your team second once the basics are in place.

Leading Workshops to Teach Daily Leadership

Daily Leadership is a skill that your consultant will teach using multiple modes including training sessions, role-playing to practice the skills, and mentoring in a live environment. Note: This could also be part of your leadership development engagement.

Teaching Problem Solving

Like the Daily Leadership workshops, problem solving is a skill that your consultant will teach via training sessions, role-playing to practice the skills, and mentoring in a live environment.

Remember the earlier discussion about tools versus principles. Use caution in your Lean consulting engagement to be sure that your consultants are able to work at a strategic implementation level and help you develop your production system and describe the specific projects, their sequence, and the value they will deliver.

WHY YOU SHOULD CONSIDER LEAN CONSULTING SUPPORT

I'm sure you've heard that the only thing constant is change. While the world is changing around your company, you have to also jump on the change wagon or risk falling behind your competitors. This is certainly true for applying Lean Thinking to improve your processes.

Be sure you have bona fide Lean experts to guide your Lean implementation. The right consultant will be skilled in leadership and culture elements, in addition to having Lean expertise, so the process will be easier to implement because you are addressing the people dynamic as you go. You will also have a better success rate in sustaining results versus if you just had someone help you implement some Lean tools.

Any change program may be overwhelming to both the leadership team and the staff that lives within the process. This is especially true for full Lean transformation initiatives. You want to make sure your consultant has been through change programs in a similar order of magnitude and knows what it's like to lead these transformations.

COSTLY MISTAKES WHEN CHOOSING A LEAN CONSULTANT—AND HOW TO AVOID THESE MISTAKES

Mistake 1: Not confirming where the consultants gained their Lean experience

When interviewing any consultant, it is important to understand exactly where they learned their Lean principles and methods. Ask them which sensei helped master their technique. Their experience in applying Lean principles is crucial so check that they are not just theoretical academics, but have actually led Lean implementations and achieved transformational results.

Mistake 2: Choosing a consultant who has not had enough leadership experience in implementing Lean

There are different processes by which consultants draw experiences from. Choosing someone who has not had a leadership role driving a full, Lean-based transformation, or who has not served as a facilitator/trainer under a leader who was driving the transformation (their "right hand") could offer suboptimal or, worse, disastrous results.

Ask your potential consultant where they have implemented Lean, and what their role was during the process (many team members claim credit, yet they were really just tertiary members, not leaders of a past transformation).

Mistake 3: Hiring a kaizen facilitator, rather than a deep Lean expert

It is easy to have someone come in and facilitate a kaizen event that is structured with a team, a well-defined scope, and aggressive but achievable goals. But, how do you know if your kaizen event is properly scoped, has the right goals, or is even for a part of your process that your strategy determines is important to improve? Many "kaizen only" consultants are unable to provide strategic help in applying Lean expertise.

Ask your consultant about kaizen events and how they know what areas would be good candidates for improvement. Check that they are tying improvement activity to provide strategic impact. Also, see if kaizen is the only approach they use or if they are comfortable with other improvement approaches as well.

SUMMARY POINTS

Here is a summary of important points to take away after reading this chapter:

- Lean Thinking, principles, and tools are incredibly powerful and, when used strategically, can be a game changer for your business
- You probably need consulting support to fully capitalize on the potential that implementing Lean Thinking, principles, and tools has for your company
- Not all Lean consultants are equal. Watch out for those who only facilitate kaizen events and seek out those that are also strategic and can take your business to the next level, with Lean within their core set of guiding principles and approach
- Know the value your consulting partner will deliver, and make your decision based on the highest potential return on investment rather than selecting a low-price resource

Watch the bonus video for this chapter at the companion website for this book:

http://www.TheStopWastingMoneyBook.com

18

Other Possible Business Transformation Consulting Engagement Topics

In this chapter, I'll review some other elements of a business transformation that could be part of the work you take on with support from your consulting partner. Specifically, I'll discuss Teamwork, Organization Structure, Problem Solving, IT Systems, and the Shingo Prize and other Programs to Award Your Business Transformation.

TEAMWORK

Building teamwork is important for any company. When teamwork is high, you can expect your company to flourish in areas of productivity, morale, and the quality of deliverables.

By teamwork we are referring to the natural interactions among groups of people who work together in their job assignments. These could be people who work for the same supervisor or manager, it could be there interactions across different departments, and it can also refer to a cross-functional team that has been created for a short-term project with team leaders and team members. In all of these cases, it's important for these teams to work effectively. A company is not a group of individuals on a roster of employees, but is one large team with many sub teams within it.

The reason teamwork is important in business transformation is because team-based approaches for implementing your strategy and your process improvement work are usually more effective than assigning individuals to specific tasks. Therefore, the area of teamwork might naturally fall under one of the other areas where you choose to use a consultant. With that in mind, it is important to consider the consulting skill sets that your consulting partner has around the elements of creating high impact and high performance teams. If it turns out that your consulting partner for other areas of your business transformation do not have the skill sets required to improve teamwork in your business, then you might be best to seek an additional consultant to help train, facilitate, mentor, and guide your team processes.

Team building requires far more than just creating fun activities that encourage collaboration and resolve issues among employees. A third-party consultant skilled in critical thinking and problem solving can help create activities and processes that meet the needs of the company that produces results. The team-building process offers team members a way to observe and analyze activities and behaviors that impede group performance and involve them in developing the course of action to overcome the problems they're experiencing. Management plays a crucial role in encouraging equal participation and making the group feel comfortable and valuable. Their attitude toward the team building process will affect the attitudes of the other team members. If management is skeptical or not on board, team building and improvement initiatives will not work.

A consultant's job will be successful in team-building activities if they are able to communicate well, successfully manage conflict, hold people accountable, establish clear goals, ensure there are adequate skills and resources, and develop trust among everyone. They are not only there to orchestrate activities and give advice, they must fully understand the underlying issues in the company that are causing the undesirable outcomes and systematically devise solutions that will have a lasting effect. The consultant must understand how the team makes decisions, functions, and communicates with each other.

ORGANIZATION STRUCTURE

Related to teamwork is the exercise to make sure you have the right people on the team in the first place, and that they are in the best-fit roles. Your organization structure is an enabler to you delivering your strategic goals by mobilizing the right skills aligned with your core values and desired culture to effectively and efficiently get the job done.

It's possible that your organization structure is not aligned in the best way to deliver the results that you are looking to achieve. It might be that your current structure does not enable clear and fast communication. Perhaps it does not facilitate teamwork or that reporting structures are misaligned. It's possible that the ratio of team and team leader is out of whack. Whatever the case may be, if you need help redesigning your organization structure, your consulting partner likely has experience with other organization structure options from working with other clients and companies prior to you engaging them.

An organization structure consulting engagement can be elaborate such as developing a matrix organization for a worldwide business that has offices internationally. That would require a consulting team to conduct quite a bit of analysis and support what would be a major transition over a period of months. In other cases, organization structure support might be simply reorganizing functional departments in a single geography.

What you'll need to review and decide is whether or not the functional managers working with your human resource team have the knowledge and bandwidth to design the change and then effectively implement the new organization structure without provoking a lapse in customer performance. It's critical that internal changes are indivisible to your external customer.

There are also internal and external communication strategies that are important to execute so that everyone appreciates what the changes are and why they are being made. It's extremely important to specify roles and responsibilities. One common framework is RACI—Responsible, Accountable,

Consulted, and Informed. For any major decision or work practice, the RACI framework is useful to figure out who is the responsible owner, who is accountable for the result, who needs to be consulted if you are considering changes, and who needs to be informed about progress and changes that are being made.

While the human resources team does not always engage the project consulting team to help with these projects, they are almost always involved because of the nature of the human resources role. Be sure to include your HR team as you consider making organizational changes and getting consulting support to help you.

PROBLEM SOLVING

Problem solving is both a skill and a discipline that is important to have in place across your company. This is another element that may be part of any other of the consulting engagements that we have already mentioned, or it could be a stand-alone engagement.

For example, within strategy execution if the results are not matching the expectations then there is a problem solving activity that kicks in to help get progress back on track. Or some Lean improvement projects may require a vigorous problem solving approach so that you and your team can continue making progress.

A specific problem-solving engagement is likely to include your consulting partner training new skills and techniques to help your teams become good at problem solving. They will also train your leadership team so they know how to lead problem-solving exercises and ask the right challenging questions to make sure solutions are robust.

The best context for theses training discussions involves solving real problems that you have in your organization right now. The consultant can train and teach methodologies and then provide support from a coaching and mentoring standpoint, as the teams are responsible for implementing solutions using the disciplined problems solving practices.

IT SYSTEMS

Many companies consider consulting support when they need to upgrade their IT systems. Sometimes this starts from a conversation with an IT sales person that plants seeds that your IT infrastructure is lacking and you can improve your performance if you upgrade to their solution. Other times you proactively reach out for help because you recognize the deficiencies in your current systems.

Given that this book is about consulting support specifically to help your business transformation, many of the details about IT consulting do not apply to this conversation. That said, you might bump into the need to upgrade your IT systems in conjunction with other business transformation activities in order to get the most out of your solutions.

Here is a perspective about it for you to consider. With business transformation in mind, start with all of the other areas that we discussed in this book before considering an IT solution to your issues. Upgrade your leadership, shift your culture, streamline your processes, and execute your strategies well. Doing all of these things are high leverage focus areas for you to attain the value you really want for your business out of the initiatives you employ.

After you launched these initiatives and see the impact they create, then you can consider whether or not new IT systems are required, or need to be upgraded to accelerate the other initiatives that you have in play. Granted, if you are a large business and acquire another business and you want to get your IT systems on the same platform, then naturally you'll need to look at this proactively right up front.

The main caution here is avoid automating wasteful activities. The best thing is to always streamline your processes and maximize what they can deliver—and then design your IT requirements on your upgraded capabilities.

SHINGO PRIZE AND OTHER PROGRAMS TO AWARD YOUR BUSINESS TRANSFORMATION

There are a number of external third party awards that your company can win. These include the Shingo Prize, The Deming Prize, The Malcolm Baldrige National Quality Award (MBNQA), International Design Excellence Awards (IDEA), or other external certifications such as ISO9000. The value of these programs and prizes is that an external auditor will check your internal processes and results and evaluate how you perform against their criteria.

By using these sets of criteria, you might define for your internal team and resources a higher level of expectation than you have had awareness of in your company. My recommendation to you is not to attempt to win any of these awards just for the sake of the award. Rather go through the business transformation that you design starting with your strategy and let the business need dictate what areas of improvement you should be driving as a team. Then, as you execute your strategies you might find it useful to consider something like the Shingo Prize.

Winning the Shingo Prize or one of these other programs can be a huge motivator and a major point of recognition and pride for you and your team members. If this becomes important for you, recognize that there are consultants who can help streamline your path to winning these prizes.

I will reiterate my caution now: don't let the prize be the end result. Let the processes of driving legitimate value-based improvement be what it is you strive to achieve and then pursue the prize in that context. There's likely to be reams of paper work within an application that may be non-value added work for you and your company.

Be aware of the amount of extra administrative work that might be required and have clarity about your real focus and motivation. After you have done that, if this makes sense to you, then go for it, have fun, and accelerate your progress with consulting support.

SUMMARY POINTS

- Third-party consultants could be beneficial to help you with your challenges and opportunities in the areas of teamwork, organization structure, problem solving, IT, and your pursuit of external prizes.
- Consulting support for many of these elements could fall under one of the other types of engagement we've discussed in the earlier chapters, or at least the need could be identified within a different type of consulting project.
- Check to be sure that your consultant that is supporting you in one area has the expertise required to help in these other areas, as well.

Watch the bonus video for this chapter at the companion website for this book:

http://www.TheStopWastingMoneyBook.com

Section IV
The Answer to Your Biggest Question: What Actions Do I Need to Take to Ensure I Hire the Right Consultant?

This book such is full of advice, suggestions, tips, and great ideas, which means you might find your brain is swimming and you really don't know what it do next.

It's not enough to learn the long list of principles in this book—the way to gain to value from those principles is to act on them. This short section will help you to take the meaningful actions that will get you long-term sustainable transformational results for your business.

Jump in now and be ready to take Action!

19

Steps to Pick Your Consulting Partner

Now that you've read the first three sections of this book and have access to this full guide of principles and ideas for you to consider as you get ready to launch your next consulting project and select a consultant to support you, it's time to convert these principles into action so that you can realize the benefits as quickly as possible.

Here are some specific next steps to guide you to make some good decisions and initiate action:

Step 1. Consider Your Situation

Assess your company's situation right now. And also contemplate your situation as a business leader for the areas of responsibility you have within your company. Ask yourself the following questions—grab a pen and jot down the answers to help guide you.

- Where is your *biggest risk* that if something doesn't change, you can be in huge trouble?
- Where are you *stuck*? (Consider that question for your company, for you, your team, and your department.)
- Where are you *unhappy with the results* you are getting? (Consider that question for your company, for you, your team, and your department.)

- Where do you believe *you have more opportunity* than you are currently achieving? (Consider that question for your company, for you, your team, and your department.)
- Where are your *biggest challenges*? (Consider that question for your company, for you, your team, and your department.)
- Where are your *biggest frustrations*? (Consider that question for your company, for you, your team, and your department.)

Take a look at the notes you've been making as you've answered all of these questions and notice your patterns.

As you recognize the patterns, you are essentially coming up with a starting point that suggests where your biggest need for help resides on your team, in your department, and in your company.

Step 2. Review the Sections of This Book That Align with Your Biggest Need

With the answers to step #1, giving you a sense of your biggest needs, scan the table of contents and find the sections that you want to reread to appreciate how consulting support might help you with the biggest need. Be sure to mark up the sections of the book that you're now reading. Make notes in the margin, jot down specific questions, and bullet the specific steps that you are now willing to take as a result of identifying your list.

Step 3. Initiate a Conversation With a Potential Consulting Partner

Now that you know that you need consulting support, you've confirmed your biggest areas of need, and you have reviewed the sections of this book that align with the needs identified, you are ready to have a dialogue with consultants about the support you are requesting. Share with your potential consulting partner your current situation, what's frustrating you, where you have concerns about your team's, departments, or company's capabilities and outline what it is that you want to solve. Also describe your aspirations in those areas. Consulting is not just about solving problems, it's also about helping raise you and your team up to the next level. Ask them how they can support you towards achieving your goals, the approach they would suggest, and their role in supporting that approach. After your initial dialogue, review the different sections of this book once again that will give you some insight to the more detailed questions to ask so that you are totally 100% convinced that they are the right consulting partner for you. I want you to design the parameters of the best consulting arrangement that will maximize your return on investment.

Step 4. Read the Next Chapter About the *Win Holistic Transformation Model*™ to Make Sure You're Thinking is Not Incomplete or Limiting Your Potential

The model I created to describe the necessary elements for a successful business transformation is called the *Win Holistic Transformation Model*™. Let me dissect the transformation model's name for you.

- *Win*—We want to help you to win (and also because that's the name of our consulting company).
- *Holistic*—It's important to think about all the interrelated pieces within your business and within your approach that will deliver maximum results. Business transformation is not a topic where you can pick from a menu those items that feel most comfortable for you and skip others that you think will be too challenging. When you read the next chapter you will get a crash course in these business transformation principles. Don't worry, there's not too much depth here. It's enough to get you started and excited about launching your business transformation.
- *Transformation*—I want to make sure you're thinking big enough. Don't stop short of your full potential by making a few small changes along the way. Rather, understand the complete magnitude of what is possible for you and strive to make changes at that level. Transformation means that the state of your people and processes changes its core form. This is exciting!

Step 5. Ask for support

If there's' anything at all that you've read in this book that you are not clear about, what to discuss deeper, or you want to ask specific questions, then call our office at +1.860.651.6859 or email Support@CompleteBusinessTransformation.com. You can also look for answers to your most challenging questions on our website:

http://www.CompleteBusinessTransformation.com.

Watch the bonus video for this chapter at the companion website for this book:

http://www.TheStopWastingMoneyBook.com

20

Understand the Win Holistic Transformation Model™

Every company has moving parts and integrated elements that creates products or provides services. While it is tricky to understand the elements and extremely difficult to systematically transform your company's processes and results, be assured that it is possible. I created the *Win Holistic Transformation Model*™ to define the required elements for you to have in place so you can transform your business.

Our approach to helping business leaders and their teams to transform their processes and achieve outstanding results is summarized by this model.

This image shows graphically the various cohesive elements for you to consider as you launch your major improvement initiatives.

WIN HOLISTIC TRANSFORMATION MODEL™

The Win Holistic Transformation Model™ provides a framework to understand what creates *Sustainable, Transformational Results*. The components include:

- Business alignment through clear ***Purpose, Vision, Mission, and Goals***
- A supportive ***Culture***

- *Core elements* to have in place to guide your transformation:
  - *Strategy Engagement Execution™ (SEE™)*
  - *Science of Success*
  - *Lean Thinking*
  - *Conscious Leadership™*
  - *Winning Team*

The Win Holistic Transformation Model™ outlines every aspect to have in place to guarantee a successful full-business transformation. It's about changing behavior and the culture (more than implementing the tools), and creating a supporting infrastructure to help guide change management and sustainable results. Transformation is an ongoing process that requires implementing the principles of success and goal achievement and gets your team into recognizing and getting excited about the possibilities. You want to ensure your transformation efforts are tied to strategic goals with clear, ongoing ACTION. Form and engage your teams, and you will have fun achieving breakthrough levels of results.

We discussed all the components of this model throughout this book, even if it wasn't obvious at the time that they assemble into a cohesive framework. Here's a quick synopsis of each component and a reminder why they are critical to include for your business transformation and how your consulting partner can help you.

Purpose, Vision, Mission, and Goals

If your company has any confusion about your purpose (why you are in business), vision (what it looks like when you are achieving your company's purpose), mission (what is your company on the planet to do—how it delivers its purpose), or its strategic goals that will make your purpose, vision, and mission a reality, then pause all other activity until you get these clear for your company decision makers. That includes your executive leadership team and all other influential leaders throughout your organization. Your consulting partner can facilitate deep discussions and lead exercises in a workshop with your senior leadership. When we lead these exercises for clients, we blend right brain with left-brain and unconscious with conscious mind to make sure the leadership team comes up with the best possible answer.

A Supportive Culture

Your culture can be a source of competitive advantage, just as Zappos declares for their business. Before you ensure your culture supports you, you have to make some important decisions about what you want your culture to be. Review Chapter 16 about Culture Shifting and the potential process by which your consulting partner can support you. Your culture is critically important to address because just as it can be a competitive advantage for you it can also completely halt your progress if its attributes do not align with your purpose, vision, mission, and goals. This is your opportunity to be deliberate about what you want your culture to be. You'll notice from our model that we list out the culture attributes of Continuous Improvement, Engagement, Action Oriented, and Trust Based. While these four attributes are a great place to start, you should expand and personalize this list to be exactly what you want to experience in your culture.

Strategy Engagement Execution™ (SEE™)

Our Strategy Engagement Execution™ process converts your strategic goals into real results and covers the content in Chapter 14 about strategy execution. Within this process are methods to engage your extended team so that you leverage and involve your organization in executing your strategies. The SEE™ creates tremendous focus and alignment within your company on your priority initiatives. For this reason, it is one of the first major exercises we help clients to install. It also offers flexibility to support any type of strategic goal and the supporting initiatives, which make this process a solid backbone for your other business transformation activities.

Science of Success

In studying the habits and practices of the most successful business leaders, entrepreneurs, athletes, and historical figures, there is a set of success principles that they tend to follow. We call this collective group of principles the Science of Success. They include elements of biology and physics, and can have a direct impact on your team's ability to develop powerful success habits themselves. Within our various client engagements, we put these principles into action as part of our interactions with client team members. Additionally, we might conduct workshops to directly teach these principles to large groups of client resources. This augments all of our other engagements and can accelerate results for our clients.

Lean Thinking

Chapter 17 went into great detail about what Lean is and how to implement Lean principles. The important thing to recognize is that Lean Thinking applies in all areas of your business, not just in your operations processes. Our consulting resources have deep experience with Lean Thinking, especially in the context of a Complete Business Transformation. This is helpful for your major lean initiatives as well as recognizing improvement opportunities within other engagements through the lens of Lean Thinking that other consultants might not see.

Conscious Leadership

In Chapter 15, we described leadership and leadership development support. With this in mind, we created a leadership model that we believe maximizes leadership effectiveness and team impact. Conscious Leadership is the next step in leadership development. It builds an emotional intelligence and describes how a leader can develop a higher conscious awareness of themselves and of other people they impact. As leaders learn to most proficiently lead themselves, they can then more effectively lead others.

Winning Team

Teamwork was part of Chapter 18. The first thing to recognize is that team-based approaches usually outperform individuals trying their best. For that reason we often guide teams and help them achieve their aggressive goals. We are expert facilitators and develop team leaders, facilitators, and members to play their roles and maximize the team's experience and performance. The other thing to recognize about teams is the organization structure and ensuring the right people are in the correct roles. Your consulting partner can advise you on the most efficient and effective organization structure, can help you evaluate success factors and get the right people into the roles where they can contribute the best, and can even help in your interviewing process for candidates for critical roles.

My main point of including this chapter about The Win Holistic Transformation Model™ is to open your mind about all the integrated pieces for you to strive to put in place. Now that you have an overview of this model, you can make some important decisions about how to get started with the improvement initiatives for your company.

Watch the bonus video for this chapter at the companion website for this book:

http://www.TheStopWastingMoneyBook.com

Conclusion

Wrap-up Thoughts and Motivation for YOU to Launch Your Next Major Business Transformation Initiatives

This book is meant to serve as an educational guide for you to digest over time. You picked it up in the first place because you had some curiosity about finding the best consulting firm to partner with you and to guide your business transformation. I'm glad you made it to the end of the book to read all four sections. If you read every page up to here then you've had quite an education, and I hope you feel equipped to hire a great consultant to support you as you transform your business.

If you're one who skimmed the book and jumped to a few sections that caught your eye as subjects relevant to your current situation, know that's perfectly fine! In fact, you made very good use of this book as the helpful resource I designed it to be. Over time as you have other challenges, you can come back and browse through again to quickly get smart about choosing a consultant for the new challenges that will emerge as you continue to progress and define higher aspirations for your business.

Most importantly, we are confident that you can achieve great results. We know how intimidating it can be to launch a series of major initiatives—we have participated in many of them ourselves. For you to go forward with conviction, you might decide to seek help from an external expert as a consultant to guide you, which will make you and your team more confident and increase your probability of success.

When you pick the right consultant to help you create huge profits and deliver long term return on investment, you can be assured that your future will improve greatly.

For You Fast Decision-Makers

Here is the fastest way to get support right away

Give us a call and allow us to assess your situation. We can guide you and provide our honest assessment of whether we are a fit to help you. Contact our office at +1.860.651.6859 or send an email to Support@ CompleteBusinessTransformation.com and we can schedule a brief chat.

About the Author

PETE WINIARSKI

Pete is a highly sought after business consultant, speaker, media guest, and international best-selling author. Pete is known as a business transformation expert and a goal achievement expert.

Having more than thirty years of experience in leadership roles, Pete leads his consulting company, Win Enterprises, LLC, to help business leaders transform their results with his team of resources who are experts in business transformation, process improvement using "Lean" principles, organization culture, leadership, and goal achievement.

His company's website, https://www.CompleteBusinessTransformation.com, is an abundant resource for business leaders to help guide their business improvement for long-term and sustainable results.

Pete is the creator of the *Win Holistic Transformation Model*™, a complete approach for companies to experience lasting transformational change. He is also the co-creator of the Conscious Leadership Model, and teaches leaders how to maximize their effectiveness as leaders of others by first leading themselves.

Pete is the author of the #1 International Best Selling book, *Act Now! A Daily Action Log for Achieving Your Goals in 90 Days*. He is also the co-author of the Best Selling books, *Elite Business Systems: Insider Strategies of Industry Leading Consultants*, *The Ultimate Game Plan: Power Up Your Consulting Business and Skyrocket Your Revenues*, and *The Innovators: Advance Your Business with Revolutionary Ideas from Today's Consulting Leaders*. Pete has contributed chapters to various other books and is in process of publishing other books on business transformation.

Pete has appeared as a business expert and a goal-achievement expert in multiple media outlets, including ABC, CBS, FOX, NBC, and Industry Week.

Pete has been trained and mentored by Jack Canfield, and is one of just a few people around the world to achieve "Certified Senior Trainer" status to deliver Jack's work with integrity and aptitude.

Pete is the co-founder of the Business Consultant Institute (http://www.businessconsultantinstitute.com) a training and mentoring firm for independent business consultants to create thriving consulting companies by delivering incredible value with high integrity.

In his spare time, Pete coaches and plays baseball, enjoys live music, and supports whatever activities his wife and two sons are pursuing.